CROSSING THE LINE

A MARRIAGE ACROSS BORDERS

LINDA VALDEZ

TCU Press
Fort Worth, Texas

Library of Congress Cataloging-in-Publication Data

Names: Valdez, Linda, author.
Title: Crossing the line : a marriage across borders / Linda Valdez.
Description: Fort Worth, Texas : TCU Press, 2015.
Identifiers: LCCN 2015026388 | ISBN 9780875656182 (alk. paper)
Subjects: LCSH: Valdez, Linda. | Valdez, Sixto. | Tucson (Ariz.)--Biogra-
phy.
  | Interethnic marriage--United States. | Mexicans--United
  States--Biography. | Immigrants--United States--Biography.
Classification: LCC F819.T953 V35 2015 | DDC 979.1/776054092--dc23
LC record available at http://lccn.loc.gov/2015026388

TCU Press
TCU Box 298300
Fort Worth, Texas 76129
817.257.7822
www.prs.tcu.edu

To order books: 1.800.826.8911

Designed by Bill Brammer
www.fusion29.com

For Lucy, the bringer of light

Author collection.

CONTENTS

Part One:
A Conversation with Pancho Villa's Death Mask

Part Two:
Life after Death

PART ONE:
A Conversation with Pancho Villa's Death Mask

CHAPTER ONE

Doña Sole didn't kill the chicken that night. She put it in the kitchen under a milk crate and put a rock on top of the crate so the bird couldn't get out. It could move around, though, pushing the crate and bumping into things. You could hear the edges of the green plastic box rub along the concrete floor. In the old days, when the floor was dirt, it would have been quieter. But not tonight. I couldn't imagine how anybody slept through the racket that bird was making.

Next to me, my husband was sleeping quite blissfully, however. On a cot next to him, our daughter Lucy added her sound-asleep breathing as testimony that comfort was possible for some this night. Some family. How could they rest so easy when I was wide awake?

But the chicken was not my only companion in sleeplessness. From the next room, I could hear Doña Sole coughing into the dark.

It was a horrible ripping sound. I felt like I was violating her privacy by hearing it. She'd tried so hard to hide it all week.

I could imagine her sitting on the edge of the thin mattress that rested on metal springs held up by a metal headboard on which her son, my husband, had painted little geometric shapes when he was a boy. It wasn't her bed. She'd insisted we take her room because it was bigger; she always did that. The bed she was sitting on was in the second bedroom. It was a little higher than the bed we were in, so her feet wouldn't quite reach her old plastic flip-flops on the floor. Her hands would be gripping the mattress

3

as she tried to cough enough so that she could go to sleep.

She was making up for a day's worth of not coughing. If she knew anyone besides the chicken was awake, she'd hold back the coughing with the same force of will that she'd used to give birth to fourteen children and raise them all to adulthood in the cactus-rib and mud house that used to stand exactly where this more solid home of concrete and adobe brick now stood.

Doña Sole's devotion to her children was the reason she kept her coughing stifled or hidden during the day. She didn't want anyone to worry. It's probably more accurate to say she didn't want anyone to know. But they did.

Sixto had heard her the first day we were here. His ultra-concerned questioning was met with hand gestures designed to tamp down his worry. "*Mijo, mijo*. It's just a little *resfrío*—a cold." Since then, I'd only heard her cough late at night, when she thought we were asleep. Or maybe just a little in the daytime, when she thought we were too far away or too busy to notice.

If I'd gotten up and offered to make her some tea with honey, she would have felt discovered, betrayed by her own coughing. The tea would have been less comfort than the illusion that we didn't know anything was wrong. So I didn't get up. I didn't wake Sixto, either, though I couldn't imagine how he slept through that other noise.

There was another bang from the kitchen as the chicken jammed the crate into something metal, like the stove or refrigerator. Sixto's sleep breathing took a hitch on a high note, then resumed its peaceful rhythm. Lucy never skipped a breath. Doña Sole became still, though, as she waited to see if anyone was up. The chicken slammed her cage into something again. There were likely big bugs wandering around the floor for her to catch, and onion skins from dinner preparations. Her jail for the night was big enough to accommodate a half-dozen hens on the factory farms that supplied most of the eggs Americans ate. So I didn't feel too sorry for her. I just wished she'd settle down in her new surroundings and shut up.

Just a few hours earlier I'd joined the others in cheering her capture.

It had been an impressive display of one of the talents Sixto didn't get to use on the US side of the line.

We'd gone to Toñita's house to say goodbye. The day had included farewell stops to see Tía Chayo and her daughters, and Luz Maria, too. But mostly we'd sat under the mango trees in Toñita's back yard to drink instant coffee and be comfortable in each other's company. As the colors around us began to take on deeper intensity, we knew the gray dusk was not far away. We still had to go back to Doña Sole's and get ready for the long drive the next day. We started our final farewells. That can take awhile in Mexico, and today was no exception.

As we rose to go, Toñita told her mother to take a chicken home to make *caldo* for her cough. Doña Sole, who still thought she'd successfully hidden things from her children, downplayed the need. It was just a little resfrío, she said, and she didn't feel like caldo in this weather. But Toñita and Sixto thought chicken soup was a good idea, so Toñita went into her house to get some chicken feed.

Toñita's house was no longer the tiny structure I'd first seen more than a decade ago. The old house had been replaced—wall by wall—thanks to money carefully saved by Toñita and her husband Gavino, and dutifully contributed by her grown children. It was now a concrete and brick house, fully covered in stucco and painted a cheerful, whipped-butter yellow. Instead of cramped spaces with lumpy, windowless mud walls, Toñita now had a living room with big windows and smooth, painted walls on which to hang the oversized portraits of her grandchildren.

She emerged from the house shaking a wrinkled paper sack. Chickens began shouldering in like paparazzi, pecking for a good angle. They were all shapes and colors, including one with very short, feathery legs. Most of them didn't have names, but Toñita called this rooster *Chaparrito*—or Shorty. She joked that the bird was like the owner; Toñita is a tiny, elegant woman who wears a long ponytail high on her head. Unlike Chaparrito, however, who waddled around under brown-and-white-speckled feathers, Toñita has an air of command.

She shook the bag without handing out much feed as the birds gathered. There were red birds and birds with elegant iridescent black feathers. Toñita pointed out a large white hen that had a sagging red comb and wagging wattle.

This is the one she wanted Sixto to catch for Doña Sole's caldo. As soon as Toñita pointed it out, the bird began to edge away. Toñita tossed some feed its way, and other chickens rushed into that space. But our bird ignored temptation and continued to move toward an old truck that must have been parked in that yard since before chickens forgot how to fly. There was safety in that dusty darkness under the truck. The chicken knew it.

Sixto knew it, too. He also began moving—stealthily, without looking directly at the bird. Toñita and Doña Sole called to Sixto to hurry up. They weren't worried about spooking the bird—the chicken was already on high alert. They were having fun, snapping out directions and laughing. Sixto would be in for plenty of ribbing if he missed his chance. He ignored them.

As Sixto closed in, the bird flapped its wings and began to run. My husband made a horizontal leap. He hung in the air like a sideways ballet dancer for just an instant. Then gravity won. His belly flop produced an impressive thud and a puff of dust. Then nothing. My husband lay face down with his hands extended under the old truck. He was as flat as its four tires. And just as still.

We waited.

"¿Hijo?" his mother called.

Nothing.

"Sixto, " I called, "are you okay?"

He was perfectly still as we watched. Seconds hung like hours. He milked every bit of drama from the scene.

"Sixto?"

Then he pulled his hands out from under the truck and got up. He was holding the bird, which was unharmed but indignant.

I hooted along with my mother-in-law and sister-in-law. What a performance! This was a side of my husband I didn't see in Tucson, where getting a chicken meant going to the corner Safeway.

He handed the chicken to his mother, and began a long process of dusting himself off. Sixto has a dread of dirt on his clothing: one dog hair will send him scurrying for the lint roller. Doña Sole held the bird upside down by its feet, the way I'd seen vendors along the road carry chickens, several in each hand. She held it that way in the back seat as we drove to her house in our little city sedan.

Our daughter had spent the afternoon with sister-in-law Emilia's girls, and they rushed to surround the car when we arrived.

When Lucy opened the back door for her grandmother, Doña Sole handed her the chicken. She took it without complaint as her Mexican-raised cousins muttered the Spanish equivalent of "Oh, gross!" Lucy held the bird—right side up—firmly enough so that it did not squirm, but not tightly enough to make it squawk. The look on Doña Sole's face was 100 percent pride as she pulled herself out of the car and watched Lucy handle the bird.

They stood side by side as Lucy transferred the chicken back into her grandmother's arms, and Doña Sole asked me to take a picture.

In those predigital days, you had to let a photo gestate in the dark womb of a film canister. So I didn't know how well that picture turned out until after we got back to Tucson. When I finally saw them grinning into the setting sun, with the chicken between them, I could feel the last glow of that fading day. They radiated happiness.

It was the last picture I would ever take of them together.

Of course I didn't know that then, either.

We ate and went to bed early that night so we would be ready for the twelve-hour drive. So why wasn't I sleeping?

I had every reason to be tired.

We'd spent the week installing tile in Doña Sole's new bathroom—her first-ever, properly functioning indoor bathroom. It was the crowning achievement of a long process of bringing my mother-in-law's home into the modern age.

I needed my sleep because I would be at the wheel when we drove off in the fuzzy-eyed predawn.

We'd made the trip from Doña Sole's *ejido* outside Los Mochis—six hundred miles from Tucson—many times. Sixto insisted we leave at 5:00 a.m. The prayers of Doña Sole and the others always carried us past whatever dangers might have awaited those who were less well protected. There was no other way to explain how we survived some of those journeys.

We were traveling during Christmas break, and it was dead dark at that hour. Winter fog rising from the damp earth made it even harder to see as we drove along rural roads where the potholes were often as big as the cows that might suddenly appear in the headlights, and every little cluster of houses had a series of speed bumps designed to scare big trucks. These topes were hell on our series of little cars, including a red Toyota Corolla and two white Nissan Sentras. If you didn't see them in time, it could be a roof-banging experience.

Sixto wanted me to drive that first stretch of road. He wanted me at the wheel when we stopped at the inspection station, which came right after we turned onto the main highway headed north.

The *federales* made you drive over a *fosa*—a concrete ditch that you straddled with your car's wheels. In the dark and the fog, I was always afraid I'd misjudge and wedge half the car into that hole where an officer waited to check the underside. He was under there to look for contraband headed out of Sinaloa, which was better known north of the border for its drug cartels than for Doña Sole's hospitality.

Sixto wasn't worried about my driving. He was afraid the guy in the pit would plant something on the car so they could add us to the arrest lists that they showed to the Americans as proof of their diligence at catching drug smugglers.

I used my pidgin Spanish to tell one officer where we'd been and where we were going, and to explain that, yes, the child asleep in the back was mine. Sixto said they'd be less likely to target a native-born American woman whose Spanish was creative but understandable. Meanwhile, he would jump out of the car to let the officer in the fosa know he was being monitored.

Sixto said they would never arrest any real smugglers; the cartels paid for safe passage. Besides, in the pea-soup conditions when we hit the road, any sensible smuggler would be snug in a nice bed. That made the federales even more eager to add us to their quota of arrests. I wondered if Sixto's meddling might just make them mad enough to give us a really bad time. But it was his country, so we did it his way. I played my role of smiling and acting as cluelessly American as possible.

So far, his system had worked.

There were other checkpoints along the way, but they didn't have the fosa. There were also places where people dressed in nurses' white uniforms would stop cars and ask you to drop donations into a can that had a red cross painted on it. *Cruz Roja*—the Red Cross. Sixto said it was bad luck not to give them something, so we always did. Near Bácum, Sonora, there was usually a group of indigenous people who pulled a chain across the narrow highway to make everybody stop—robber barons without the river or the castle. But they had humble demands. A few pesos would be enough to get them to drop the chain and let you drive on.

Vendors gathered there to take advantage of the stopped traffic. They sold homemade bread and sometimes had little parrots in wooden cages. These were wild-caught birds from somewhere to the south. They looked very sad and frightened. I sometimes thought of buying them so I could turn them loose, but these birds wouldn't survive in the hard-used desert around the highway. Besides, buying one would just make the vendors catch more birds to sell. Still, I always dreamed of freeing those poor birds and watching their little green bodies disappear into some equally green forest.

Now I was just dreaming of dreaming. Or at least sleeping.

I had to get through this night.

I could hear Sixto and Lucy sleeping, their breathing unsynchronized, untroubled.

I pushed myself up on my elbows to look at Sixto's face. My mind filled in the details that I couldn't clearly see in the dark: his long eyelashes, his nose like an ancient Toltec carving, his midnight hair speckled with white even then. A beautiful man.

When we first got married, he used to bring me long-stemmed roses—bought at a high price and given with a glowing love. I said it was a waste of money. We should be thriftier. He said it felt like I'd dumped a bucket of ice water on his head. I said I was sorry. Then he stopped bringing me roses. And I was sorrier.

When I first met him, I was effervescent. I was a bubble in a just-opened bottle of Mexican Coke. Suddenly awakened, rising fast, and ready to disappear into something bigger, different. A new element. Another state of being. I emerged into another world. A place of mango trees and poinsettia bushes.

But I never let go. Never stopped being afraid of what would happen when the bubble burst. Like my comment about the roses,

I always managed to pull back from the edge of ecstasy. I always tried to hold on to my sense of control.

In this dark night, I was out of effervescence. Like a half-empty, two-liter jug of Coke from yesterday's celebration.

I just wanted to get us all home safely. I thought it was all up to me.

I could just make out Lucy's shape on the cot next to our bed. She slept as profoundly as her father, abandoning me to the night. How sharper than a serpent's tooth, I thought. But I didn't mean it; she's a good kid and a great chicken handler.

Doña Sole's big wooden wardrobe dominated the wall facing our bed. The tiny mirror on the front reflected a little light from somewhere, and I was grateful for that. I've never liked sleeping in the dark. At home, I have a night-light.

This was the only mirror in Doña Sole's house the first time I came here. I once tried to describe to a hairstylist the trials of putting on makeup and drying my hair in an eight-inch square of half-blind mirror. I was just making what I considered amusing small talk while she cut my hair. But she responded with a level of disgust that I hadn't anticipated: Who could live like that? How could you stay in such a place? Weren't there any hotels? I explained about my husband. About his mother, and how her feelings would be hurt if we stayed somewhere else. The stylist looked at me as though I might have brought back lice. At least take a mirror with you next time, she said. I did. I took several over the years.

I also found a different hairstylist.

That wardrobe was one of the places where Doña Sole stored—but never used—some of the gifts we brought to make her life easier. Thick towels, flowered sheets, tablecloths. She'd bring them out when we visited—for our use only—then wash them and put them away for the next time. No amount of coaxing could convince her to use them for herself. They were much too nice, she said.

There was a narrow space between the hulking wardrobe and the corner of the bedroom—a darker shade of black.

This is where I first saw him.

Waiting.

Pancho Villa was hovering in the corner of Doña Sole's bedroom with an air of timeless patience. It wasn't all of him. Just his head. His death mask to be exact. A grotesque image, frozen at the moment of a violent death that followed a violent life. The scraps of light in that room reflected off the high relief of the metal casting; the low spots—where his eyes should have been—were blacker than death's shadow.

I recognized that mask.

I first saw it when I walked into a room in a museum in Chihuahua City. As soon as I saw it, I wished I could return to the minute before I saw it—to the time before I entered that room. But there was no going back, no erasing that image from my mind.

The death mask was horrible for any number of reasons.

It showed the complete defeat and betrayal of a man who once had great power and self-confidence. Some artisan used skill and talent to make a model and a casting that commemorated death's triumph, life's impotence. Pancho Villa had been bigger than life; this showed him smaller than death. His face became a curiosity to scare tourists. It was unfair to do that to somebody.

As unfair as death on a sunny day.

In Tucson, we have a statue downtown of Pancho Villa on his horse. He has all the cockiness and vigor one associates with a rebel general in the Mexican Revolution. He's ready for action. You can almost hear him yell something provocative to the passing cars with their workaday drivers. Rise up, you pack of *borregos*. Show some spine, you *pollitos*.

I like the statue.

I hate the death mask. But I remembered it.

And I recognized him now in Doña Sole's bedroom.

I felt my chest tighten. I wanted to scream. But I didn't. That only works to chase away nightmares. I was awake.

I stared at the death mask. If he made a move, I'd scream. But he was in no hurry.

I thought about my options.

I could wake up Sixto. He would shine his little flashlight

around the room and show me that there was nothing there. Just a bad dream or a late-night illusion, he'd whisper, being careful not to wake Lucy.

He'd say, "Go to sleep, *mi amor*. I'll stay awake."

And he would stay awake.

Then he'd hear his mother coughing, and he'd call out to her. She'd feel discovered and be denied the comfort of being able to cough in peace.

And after Sixto went back to sleep, I'd wake up and the mask would still be there.

I very slowly put my head back down on the pillow, but I kept Pancho Villa in my sight. I tried not to be so afraid. I wanted to be somewhere else. Somewhere safe. I wanted to be someone else. Someone courageous.

But I only had this place and this time.

I sat up slowly and looked at him full on.

"Did my mother laugh in your face when you came for her?" I whispered.

My mother laughed at so many things I found terrifying. She laughed at my fear of the dark, even though she always let me keep a night-light in my bedroom. Later, when she discovered her adult daughter still slept with the light on, she laughed about how I still hadn't "gotten over that." Getting over things was her stock message, along with letting troubles "roll like water off a duck's back."

She probably did laugh. Or call him a jerk.

But acting tough didn't seem like the best approach right now. What did I think I was going to do? Scare him?

He was the scariest thing in the room.

Maybe I could talk him away. Play Scheherazade to Pancho Villa's king.

Don't laugh. My life has been about mixing metaphors and blending cultures for quite some time. Maybe I could talk Pancho Villa into leaving with just the chicken.

He was still waiting, his bruised and broken face locked forever, unhealed and un-healable, in hard metal.

"At least you should know who we are," I whispered.

At least you should know how I got here.

CHAPTER TWO

Back in 1988, my mother was on a campaign to get me to loosen up. I needed it.

Those were the days when professional women were warned in somber news stories about biological clocks and the specter of childlessness. I was in the newspaper business, so I not only read all that stuff, I believed it. I'd been told by authoritative journalists that I was more likely to get killed by a terrorist than get married. Right on cue, I began to hear my biological clock chiming twelve times across an empty landscape.

After all, I was over thirty.

It didn't take long for my boyfriend to catch on. My biggest mistake was pointing out a cute little boy in an all-you-can-eat restaurant. I heard lullabies. He heard a telltale ticktock. He didn't run out of the restaurant. But he did leave alone for the camping trip we'd been planning together.

I was left with two weeks off and a new pair of hiking boots.

My mother saw this as an opportunity.

As I sat at the dining-room table in her trailer feeling sorry for myself, she bustled around cooking dinner. I was trying to discuss whether to make a clean break of it or stay in the duplex where he and I had spent so much time over the last few years. She was trying to change the subject. She had a trip planned for those same two weeks. She was going to Mexico's Copper Canyon, and she wanted me to go with her.

"What else are you going to do with your vacation?" she asked. "Mope around and feel sorry for yourself?"

"I could find a new apartment and move," I said.

"That doesn't sound like much fun," she said.

"I'm not really in the mood for much fun," I said.

"Why not?" she said. "That's just what you need. Take your mind off your troubles. I always have a lot of fun in Mexico. You should come along."

It's worth knowing a few things about my mother, besides the fact that she could laugh in the face of danger. She also had a thing about being flexible. One of her favorite parables was about the difference between a telephone pole and a tree. The tree, she used to point out, was far less likely to break in a high wind because it could bend. Her name was LaVerne, which she told me meant "green trees," and she lived the lesson of the trees.

In 1964, she gave up her upper-middle-class, Midwest American lifestyle for something much less comfortable. I was eleven years old, and she took me to Arizona because the doctor said he had no other medicine to give me. Asthma was likely to kill me if I stayed another winter in Cleveland, he said.

My father stayed behind because there weren't a lot of jobs in Tucson for men who'd spent their lives working in the steel mills along Lake Erie. My sister, ten years my elder, decided to come West for the adventure. My brother, eight years my elder, also worked at the mill, so he stayed in Ohio.

My father sent us money every month, but it was only what he could afford after maintaining that upper-middle-class lifestyle back home. He didn't send much. My mother found us a series of affordable apartments—most of which came with large roaches and lecherous landlords. She became expert at handling both kinds of vermin.

The move had the intended effect on me. I discovered what it was like to ride a bike without winding up in the emergency room. That was a goal she'd been praying for, so she didn't complain about the decline in her lifestyle.

That first December, my father and brother came to visit. They'd been more roomies than father and son since we left. My brother was twenty and working at the steel mill with my father. They drove down in a new car that they planned to leave for us. It was a 1965 Dodge Charger. It was not the car my mother would have chosen—or the color. It was dark blue, hotter than blazes in the Tucson sun.

She grumbled about the cost. She also liked her old car—a fire-engine-red 1964 Dodge 440. They were going to drive that one back and leave her with the new one. She wasn't happy about having that decision made for her. But she didn't complain too much.

She didn't even complain about the way they betrayed her in Mexico. But that came later.

First there was the playacting at being a happy family. Everybody worked hard at this, and the strain often showed. On Sunday, we all drove down to the US-Mexico border and into Nogales, Sonora, Mexico. Even my sister went along, though at twenty-one she had far more interesting things to do than spend time with her family.

Day trips to Mexico were a tourist standard in those days. I don't think any of us ever thought about how much we looked the part of Ugly Americans. The whole thing was so overwhelming. As soon as my father pulled into a parking spot on the Mexican side, the new car was surrounded by little boys imploring with hands outstretched. They knew at least one phrase in English, and they called it out over and over: "Watch your car, Mister?"

My father gave a few of them some coins. "Insurance," he said. My mother said we should have brought the older car; this one was too much of a target. I looked with alarm at kids younger than I. Could they protect the car? And what did they need to guard it from? They seemed less like children than like miniature adults. Hard, but not in the pretend way the boys in school tried to act hard. So maybe they could do something. I hoped so. I was beginning to like the new car, despite my mother's obvious discomfort with it. I enjoyed my father's demonstration of how fast it could go on the drive down. But as we were gathering our stuff and locking up the car, the kids rushed off to surround another car as it pulled up to the curb.

"I thought they were going to watch it," I said.

My father laughed.

My mother stage-whispered to me: "We paid them so they wouldn't do something to it."

I didn't have long to think about this. The manic pace of the border-town tourist district was too distracting. Sensory overload. The streets were lined with open-front curio shops with colorful, exotic stuff spilling out onto the sidewalks. Kids not much bigger than the ones we paid not to watch our car were using English phrases to pull us in.

"Hey, Lady. I make you very good price."

"Come in, look around."

"Best prices. What you need?"

We walked past some shops and into others. The focus of the shopkeepers was intense. My mother liked to bargain. My sister liked to flirt. My brother liked the cheap leather coats. My father liked the cheap booze. They had something for everyone.

On the street corners, there were burros hooked up to colorful carts that had things like "Mexico Lindo" painted on wooden arches over the seats. My father paid for a Polaroid picture of me sitting in one of those carts and wearing a sombrero.

I could see the poverty behind the colorful trappings, but I didn't really know what it was. One kid on the street had a pair of sunglasses he'd made by shaping wire for the frame and gluing colored plastic where the lenses should be. My mother thought it showed ingenuity. My father said, "These people have no pride."

When we crossed the border to go home, we left the Third World behind. I didn't feel so confused. I liked it better after we were safely on the North American side.

But there was another side of that border town—a place taxi drivers told my father about while my mother was haggling over the price of a silver bracelet. That evening, after dinner, he announced that he and my brother were going back to Nogales the next day. He said they'd forgotten to get something, and he made it sound like he was going to buy somebody a present.

They left while I was at school the following day. My mother was at home, but she told my sister to pick me up in her MG Midget. My sister made jokes about a place called Canal Street and the girls who worked there. Prostitutes, she said.

"What?" I said.

"You better not say anything, or Mom will be really mad," she said.

My sister dropped me off at our apartment and roared off for some of her own more interesting plans. My mother and I ate together, but she didn't talk much. I was in bed by the time my father and brother brought back the new car. They were still asleep when my mother drove me to school in it the next morning.

I noticed two holes in the floor mat on my side of the car. They were each about the size of a dime, about eighteen inches apart.

"What're those?" I asked. They hadn't been there before.

"They look like heel marks," she said icily.

"Heel marks?"

"They look like holes made by spike-heeled shoes," said my mother, who never wore spike-heeled shoes.

Her tone said, *Be quiet now*. So I was.

That afternoon, my father and brother were with my mother when she came to get me from school. My father was unusually cheerful, but he was the only one. The Al Martino song "Spanish Eyes" came on the radio. "Prettiest eyes in all of Mexico," Martino crooned. My father turned up the radio and sang along loudly: "Please, say sí, sí. Say you and your Spanish eyes will wait for me."

My brother was slumped down in the front passenger seat. From the back seat, my mother said to him, "I'll bet you can tell me what happened to the floor mat."

No answer. She reached over the seat and turned down the radio.

"I wonder what makes you like that song so much," she said to my father.

He didn't respond. But he wasn't cheerful anymore.

So that's how my father betrayed my mother in Mexico. It took me a while to put things together, but I eventually figured it out. Our family went on like that for another five years.

My mother, sister, and I spent the winters in Arizona while my father worked in Ohio and sent us money. He supported us. That made him a good father, my mother said. My mother always pointed that out when I protested our annual summer drive back to a place my father erroneously called "home." My sister was old enough to opt out of the summer trips, and she wisely did so.

It was left to my mother and me to discover each new outrage when we arrived at the red brick house she used to call her "dream house."

One year, my mother found her cookbooks and boxes of recipes gone. They burned them in the fireplace out back, my father told her. No reason given. Another year, her family pictures had been stuffed into a damp basement cupboard. They were moldy, so she ordered me upstairs so the smell wouldn't trigger an asthma attack. I heard her feed them into the incinerator, one memory at a time. My father had never liked her family. One year, many of the stamps in my grandfather's extensive collection had been pried off the pages of the books into which he had carefully mounted them. My mother figured they'd been sold, but nobody would admit anything. One year, the basement had been turned into a shooting gallery for real guns.

The next year, when I was sixteen, my father died. My mother asked me to draw a picture of a saguaro cactus. She had this carved into his headstone, along with the words "A little bit of Arizona." He'd loved the desert, she said, but he continued working in Ohio so we could live in Arizona.

"He wasn't perfect," she said, "but he was your father, and he always provided for you. That's more than a lot of men do."

My father used to joke that my mother would be a "rich widow" if he died first. But the steel company found a way to deny his retirement benefits. She sold the house, paid off his stack of high-interest loans, and we became full-time Arizonans.

My mother bought a twelve-by-sixty-foot trailer because she was tired of landlords telling her what to do. Then she got tired of trailer-park managers telling her what to do, so she bought an acre of cheap land ten miles out of town and parked the trailer between four mesquite trees. By that time, I was living on my own, and I thought she was crazy for moving so far from town.

She lived there, and slept in the dark, even after a man she knew broke in and raped her at gunpoint. It was her gun. She'd pulled it out of the drawer and fired it as he came in the window. Of course, she missed. That's when he took it away and held it to her head while he assaulted her.

He was still there the next morning when I drove out for a visit. I didn't have a phone in my apartment, so she hadn't been able to call me. I could tell something was wrong when I got there.

He was trying to make amends by working in the front yard. My mother was going along, trying to figure out how to get rid of him without getting hurt again. While he worked, she took me into the bedroom and showed me the bullet hole in the dresser and explained what happened. She didn't want to call the police, so I stayed at her side until he left.

I insisted she and her dog come into town to stay at the house I shared with a girlfriend. After a few days, she went home, saying nobody—nobody—was going to chase her away from her place.

He came back once or twice, driving slowly down the road, but not stopping to open the gate at the end of the long driveway. I wondered how she managed to get through the dark nights so far from the city. She said God would take care of her. The fact that God had apparently been on holiday the last time she needed help didn't faze her. It was a case of mind over matter, she told me. She was going to stay at home.

About a year later, there was another incident with a gun. This time, it involved me, and it nearly destroyed me.

I got into a screaming argument with a young man that I loved very much. He walked out of the duplex where I was living, pulled his gun out of the glove compartment of his van, and shot himself in the forehead. I was twenty years old. When the police asked who they should call, I gave them my mother's number. She came for me.

As we drove on the long dark highway to her place, I kept repeating, "I hope he knows I love him, and I hope he knows I'm sorry." She said she was sure he knew those things.

It was late when we got to her trailer. She dug a night-light out of the junk drawer and plugged it in. I asked if I could sleep with her, and she said, "Of course." I asked if I could hold her hand, and she said, "Of course."

My sister came down from Flagstaff to take me to the funeral. It was a nice gesture, but we got in a fight because she brought a white dress. I'd spent the whole previous day going from store to store looking for a suitable plain black dress. I even had a black veil for my head. I told her she looked like she was going to a party; she said white was the color of mourning in many countries. She wouldn't change, so we drove off—black and white—to say goodbye to a young man whose death shattered my spirit.

It was ten years later when I finally left my mother's trailer and got another place of my own. By then, I'd finished my BA on a federal grant and gotten a job at a newspaper. During my college years, I'd had a Lebanese boyfriend who made me cry when he left to go home, and a German boyfriend who did the same. My mother suggested maybe I should try a nice American boy for a change. One who wouldn't leave. So I did.

Now that he'd walked out on me, my mother was on a campaign to get me to go to Mexico with her.

"I'm sure we can squeeze you in," she said, placing a plate of pork chops in mushroom gravy, potatoes, and green beans on the table in front of me.

When I hesitated, she rushed to the other room to call the tour guide. She'd been on a series of trips south with this guide, a Mexican woman who arranged economical trips for Americans on a budget. The guide's philosophy was that travel should be well lubricated with margaritas. My mother always came home glowing with stories of days filled with amazing sights and nights floating on tequila and dancing.

She was smiling when she returned from her phone call: not only was there space for me, I'd have my own room at no extra charge. She was already sharing her room with her long-time friend Dottie. So I'd have no roommate!

I agreed—reluctantly—to go with her.

We were originally supposed to fly to Los Mochis, Sinaloa, where we would catch the train that would take us through Copper Canyon. But the employees of Aeromexico went on strike the week before we were scheduled to leave. Not to worry, said our guide. She'd arrange for us to take a nice, air-conditioned bus for a comfortable twelve-hour ride. I pictured a private coach with darkened windows, a movie, and a really tidy bathroom.

Instead we boarded an old bus that looked like the butt of every joke my father ever told about Mexicans. There was orange fringe around the windshield and a faded, once-red velvet cloth on the dashboard. Mounted on one side of the dash was a statue of the Virgin of Guadalupe. On the other side was one of those chrome silhouettes of a busty woman with a pencil waist. The driver gave me the old up-and-down body scan as I climbed aboard his bus. Having been recently dumped, I found myself secretly grateful. This guy was obviously a connoisseur of the feminine.

Our tour guide arranged for us to board first and occupy the seats at the front. After that, people poured in, packing all the remaining seats and filling the aisle. When the driver finally shut the door of the bus and pulled into the street—without pausing for any oncoming traffic—the bus held more people than I would have thought possible. Amid the babble of Spanish, I could hear our guide several seats up deflecting questions about the air-conditioning—there wasn't any—with talk of an icy pitcher of margaritas waiting at the end of the line.

It was a blast-furnace June day on the Sonoran Desert. But the windows were open and the hot air was dry enough to evaporate any sweat before it had a chance to bead. We were on our way, and judging from the number of people still in line when the bus door was slammed shut, we were among the lucky ones.

The bus stopped frequently to exchange passengers. Sometimes there was nothing but a hopeful group of people waiting at a crossroad in the middle of nowhere. Sometimes we made more formal rest stops where we could get off to buy a soda and visit a tiny bathroom hidden behind a gas station. Sitting at a table just outside the door would be an old woman with a roll of toilet paper and money box. For a few pesos, you got a couple of sheets and the nod to go inside. Those who anticipated the need for more toilet paper had to pay extra.

As we moved farther away from the hyperventilating border town, Mexico seemed to take a deep breath and remember that it was supposed to be a gracious and unhurried place. I developed a Zen-like relationship with the heat, and during one rest stop, I looked out over a rolling desert and wondered why I had never done this before. I liked this calmer Mexico. The people here weren't desperate and harried the way they were in the frontier along the border. There was more space here. More time.

As we rode toward sunset, I was dreaming of how nicely the

desert air always cools off after nightfall—especially when you are far from the city. I imagined how that night air would pour through the open windows, fresh and dry. There was the promise of comfort down the road.

But as we left the ranch country of Sonora and headed toward the agricultural lands of Sinaloa, we also left the desert behind. In an instant, the air changed into the kind of humid, sticky stuff crop plants like. It came through the windows and hit my face like a sour, wet washcloth. I was trying hard to find the Zen in the sultry night when the bus began to slow for yet another stop.

We pulled into a relatively large bus station in a place called Navojoa, on the southern edge of Sonora and just two hours from our destination. Fluorescent lights buzzed from poles high above the station as two men climbed on the bus. The aisles were clear now; we'd left the big crowds behind. The journey had a short-timer feel. We'd be at the hotel soon and could enjoy the air-conditioning that our tour guide assured us would be working just fine at the Hotel Santa Anita, the finest hotel in Los Mochis. I was looking forward to an icy shower and some crisp sheets as the bus pulled back onto the highway.

The two men who got on at Navojoa brushed past on their way to the front of the bus. It wasn't unusual for people to get off between towns, so I didn't think anything of it. But these guys didn't wait at the steps for the bus to stop. Instead, they turned to face the passengers, pulling bandannas over their noses as they did so. One held a pillowcase and a large kitchen knife. His partner, who waved a gun, yelled something in Spanish. The rest of the bus snapped to attention and gasped. Our tour guide hiked up in her seat and hissed back at us in English: "This is a robbery." The English speakers snapped to attention and gasped.

After some heated dialogue, the driver handed over the blue plastic zipper bag where he'd been putting the money he collected from those who got on between bus stations. The gunman stuffed it into his shirt and stood watch as the guy with the pillowcase strode to the back of the bus. He worked his way forward, demanding money as he went. There was a lot of rustling and mumbling and an occasional loud grunt or shout from the robber. The kids on the bus were quiet for the first time, even the babies. The gunman at the front was growling to the driver, who kept the bus barreling down the unlit highway.

When the pillowcase collection reached my aisle, I put in all my cash: sixty dollars. My mother shoved a bill into the sack, looked at the robber, and shrugged. He looked at me again and I started reaching for my Travelers Cheques. My mother leaned over me, pinning my hand in my purse, and shrugged her shoulders theatrically at the robber. Nothing more here. They looked at each other. She raised her eyebrows. He moved on.

"You don't need to give him everything," she hissed at me.

She had given him a five-dollar bill.

When the collection was over, one of the robbers said something to the driver, who seemed to be in a trance. He just kept driving. The gunman yelled a few times, then fired a shot into the floor of the bus. The driver slammed on the brakes and threw open the door. After they got out, the driver sat there—once again in his very personal space—looking into the dark field that had embraced the robbers and our money.

People began yelling at him to move. He drove a few hundred meters without shutting the door and stopped again. Everybody started calling out—in Spanish and English—drive on, *adelante*. Go, for Pete's sake. He was still staring out the open door. We yelled. Louder and louder. Then, suddenly, he snapped the door shut and drove away.

The bus was a cacophony of English and Spanish. People spit their outrage and assessed the damage. Kids whined. Babies wailed.

Yet each turn of the wheel took us a little farther away from danger. If we just kept going, we would arrive safely at our destination. We were safe inside the bus. The motion kept us safe.

That sense of security lasted about ten minutes.

Then a military checkpoint came into view. It consisted of a small building surrounded by soldiers with big guns. There was no barrier across the road, and the federales didn't look interested in stopping anybody. The Mexican passengers called out to the driver, telling him not to stop. There was an intensity in these voices that was contagious. We started yelling, too. Don't stop.

But he did.

The bus shuddered as he downshifted too fast and pulled into the dirt lot. Banging open the door, he slouched off the bus toward the office with the air of a condemned man. It seemed like only seconds after he reached the yellow light of that little office that the federales came running over to order us all off the bus. Their guns looked bigger close up, and the soldiers looked younger. They were just boys.

We were the most interesting thing to happen on that road in a very long time.

The passengers stood in little groups outside as they searched the bus, poking at the luggage in the overhead shelves. Nobody knew what they were looking for. Nobody asked. A woman had left her baby sleeping in one of the seats, and the child let out a terrified scream. An officer who looked like he should be in junior high school stopped the mother as she tried to run back on the bus. She shouted at him as the baby screamed. He stood aside. The officers who'd done the searching—and awakened the baby—followed as she carried her child off the bus.

Now it was time to question the passengers.

They began moving among the clusters of Mexican passengers. The officers nodded and adjusted their assault weapons as people told their stories. None of them wrote anything down. One soldier came over to us, and our tour guide stepped forward to translate. She turned many of our simple one- or two-word responses into long explanations that included back-and-forth exchanges between her and a young officer. She didn't immediately translate all of this for us, and I wasn't able to follow much. I could tell that the soldier was trying to be professional. Our guide was undermining this by repeatedly calling him mijo and cajoling him into saying more than he'd intended.

After he moved on, she gathered us around her and explained in conspiratorial tones that the federales suspected the driver was behind the robbery. After all, the robbery occurred near the end of the run, when the cash bag would be fullest. We all nodded in an ah-ha sort of way—even though anyone who knew the daily schedule could have figured out the best time to commit a robbery. It was clear that our group was ready to throw the driver under the bus. I didn't know how the Mexican passengers felt about it.

We could all see the driver through the open door of the office. He was sitting in a chair surrounded by armed interrogators who were all young enough to be his grandsons. He shook his head dramatically and looked from one to another.

My mother and Dottie were utterly unconcerned. They were chattering with the rest of the group about what a good story this would make when they got home. Even our guide didn't seem ready to consider the very real problem we would face if our driver were arrested—or if he decided to tell the federales that the robbers had accomplices among the passengers. I thought the Mexican passengers understood, though. Like me, they kept watching the office to monitor the driver's interrogation.

The children and babies were quiet again, like they'd been during the robbery. The danger had not passed. It had just shifted from two men with a small gun to a bunch of kids with big guns.

The night was so hot you could hear the stones in the parking lot sweat. The star-studded sky should have been dazzling. But outside the circle of light we were in, the black walls of night were so sinister that the stars looked like spies. We were one hundred miles outside of nowhere. I wouldn't call the place God-forsaken because I didn't want to preclude help from above. We might need divine intervention.

Then it was over.

The driver rushed out of the office and climbed into the bus without a word. We scrambled to get in as he gunned the engine. He was already pulling away when the last man jumped on. As we drove away, the young boys of the Mexican Army lounged against the building, laughing, with their guns slung over their shoulders. They had let us go. But they had the firepower to do anything they wanted, and the uniforms to make it legal. We knew it, and so did they. The driver did not stop again. He barely even slowed down when we reached Los Mochis city traffic.

We arrived at the Hotel Santa Anita well after midnight. Our guide convinced the driver to stop right in front of the hotel. As I passed the bookends of womanhood on his dashboard, I wondered which one gave him more comfort when he was negotiating his fate with the federales in that little office. I'd been rooting for him, but he didn't have an icon to celebrate anybody like me.

We stepped off the bus into another Mexico.

This hotel had the kind of spit-and-polish presentation that's only possible in a country where labor is cheaper than chewing gum. Eager young men rushed out to take our luggage and carry it to the front desk, where a smiling young woman was happy to check us in. This place was bright and safe, and the air-conditioning worked great. I headed for my room. My mother, Dottie, and the rest of the Greatest Generation babies headed into the bar for those margaritas they'd been hearing about all day.

I called my newspaper to report the robbery—they did a little research on that end and ran a story saying no Mexican state, local, or federal authorities had heard about the event that we had dutifully stopped to report to the federales. I'd done my duty. After a shower, I let the cool sheets caress me to sleep.

I was awakened by a woman screaming.

As I sat up in bed, staring at the bolted door, I began to realize this had more to do with margaritas than bloody murder. I heard Dottie apologizing profusely in Spanglish. She'd walked into the wrong room. Some murmurs were cut short by a slamming door. Dottie was still apologizing to the empty hallway when I opened my door. About that time, my mother stepped into the hall from a few doors down and called out, "Dottie, over here." Dottie gave me a giggled goodnight and rushed off. As I got back in bed, I looked at the clock. It was past three.

By the time we boarded the train, I was just counting the days until I'd be home safe in my own apartment.

"Don't be so serious," my mother told me. "Nobody's gonna rob the train."

Oh, yeah?

She insisted I take the window seat on the *Chihuahua al Pacífico* train—*el Chepe,* they called it—though I had no idea what that meant. My mother wanted me to relax, enjoy myself, and look at the scenery. She and Dottie, on the other hand, didn't stay seated long enough to look at the view, let alone appreciate it. They were buzzing about, talking to other members of our group or hanging out in the next car with our tour guide, who had a thermos of iced margaritas and lots of juicy stories about the people who worked at the hotel we'd just left and the one where we would stay tonight.

I watched as we passed countless little villages nestled between great expanses of cropland. The homes were part of local *ejidos*, those communal farms that were a long-ago land reform by a progressive government seeking to give the poor a stake in their country and their future. If the goal of the ejido system had been prosperity for all, the failure was obvious. Most of the houses were made of mud or tarpaper with roofs of black plastic held down with rows of rocks along the perimeter. Outhouses were patched together with scraps and old campaign signs. Those signs were sturdy building material, sure. But there was a hint of playfulness in the pragmatism of repurposing these campaign promises. The sight of grinning politicians tacked upside down on outdoor privies was a pungent political statement.

There was artistry, as well.

Behind the three-strand barbed-wire fence that separated the tracks from the homes, people had built corrals from mesquite logs, wire, and creativity. One enclosure consisted of the metal interior of box-spring mattresses stood end to end. The exposed and rusted coils created a repeating pattern that arched gracefully up over a small hill and contained a group of thin goats.

As the train passed, men stopped what they were doing to watch. Old women in simple cotton dresses draped laundry over the barbed wire to dry. Young women emerged from mud huts in fine dresses, high heels, and drop-dead gorgeous hairdos. Behind them came little girls in impossibly white dresses and little boys in pressed black suits and perfect bow ties.

Some of the houses looked ready to fall over or melt in the next hard rain. Others were solidly built of cinder blocks and painted bright colors. All of them had one thing in common. The front doors were open.

When the yard was full of people seated on chrome-legged kitchen chairs and sipping coffee, the front door was open. If the only person around was an old woman sweeping the dirt yard, the front door was open. When uniformed children rushed home from school, they ran in an open front door. If the yard was empty except for a skinny brown dog and a few chickens, the front door was still open. Even if the only sign of life was smoke rising from a fire out back, the front door was open.

My imagination tried to pass the threshold into the dark interiors. What went on in those houses? How did those young women make themselves look so good without running water? How did mothers keep their kids clean? How did the old women wash the clothes?

There was something more than poverty in these houses that were patched together out of recycled materials and broken political promises. Nothing in my experience prepared me to understand what motivated people to dress their little girls like princesses when they lived like peasants. This was Third World poverty. But the poor weren't behaving as I'd expected.

They polished their children like jewels, and they sparkled through the dust. They made the dust blossom, too. Bougainvillea of all colors climbed across the roofs of ratty little shacks. Queen Anne's wreath created pink walls around mud huts. People used old plastic tubs, empty coffee cans, and tires as pots for ferns and dieffenbachia so lush they almost didn't look real. This was a different kind of poverty.

For hours we passed those houses, and I tried to see inside those open front doors. But I couldn't see beyond the darkness. Then we began to enter the canyon country, with amazing railroad bridges spanning deep gorges and long tunnels that you could see from miles away. The train snaked along at vacation pace. Little by little this trip began to feel like a good idea again. By late afternoon, the train stopped at a hotel deep in Tarahumara canyon country. We would be there until we caught the train going the other direction at noon the next day. The hotel was called Posada Barrancas. When I stepped off the train, the air was cool and it had a clean, high-desert smell that made the rest of the world seem musty and in need of a good shake. The Tarahumara weave beautiful baskets, and if you put your face into one of those baskets—even years after putting it on a shelf in Tucson—you can still smell the canyon.

The train station was just a landing with an awning, and this was just a quick stop to exchange passengers. There was a bustle of anxiety while everyone in our group accounted for his or her luggage. Everyone except Dottie.

Her bag had been lost on the first leg of the journey—between Tucson and Nogales. She'd been hoping it would catch up with her—something everyone else saw as an entirely unjustified expectation. But Dottie needed some hope. Her daughter had died six months earlier, leaving behind Dottie's son-in-law and two grandsons. She had been Dottie's only child, and Dottie still talked about her in the present tense—especially after a few margaritas. My mother had convinced her old friend—as my mother had convinced me—that this trip would be the best thing for her. Dottie mostly kept her pain to herself, though she talked too much about everything else.

She confided a new need to me as we walked down the long pathway to the hotel complex.

"Honey," she said, "you know I hate to bother you. I can't ask your mother. She's done so much for me already. She's just wonderful, you know I think the world of her."

I nodded and Dottie went on.

"I know you speak Spanish—of course you do, you're so clever. Your mother is so proud of you. I can speak some Spanish, of course, because my second husband was Mexican, but he always wanted to speak English. He never would teach me a word of Spanish. Not one word." Here she laughed in that ragged, forced way of hers. It was more about self-deprecation than mirth, but it must have served her well over the years. She punctuated much of her speech with it.

"Uh-huh," I said. I'd heard about the Mexican husband before and was hoping the conversation would not go off on this tangent. I wasn't really tired. I just wanted to keep thinking about the mysteries of those houses.

For once, Dottie was direct: "Honey, I need your help."

"Okay," I said, "what can I do?"

She explained about the lost luggage—which I already knew. She said she didn't mind washing out her underwear every night, and that my mother had given her a spare toothbrush (my mother would have a spare toothbrush) and let her borrow some clothes.

"Even if they are too small, but I would never complain," she said.

"Of course not."

"Honey, there's just one thing I can't get along without. I can't ask our guide because she has to help everybody and get the margaritas ready," she laughed again, this time with an almost manic sense of anticipation.

"What can I do for you, Dottie?"

"You're so wonderful," she said again. "I just hate to ask."

"It's no problem. What can I do?"

"Honey, you're wonderful. If you could just spare a minute—I know you are busy, you have so many things to do. I just need a minute. Please help me out. Just say you will. There's just one thing I can't get along without . . . "

The thing she needed—the one thing she couldn't get along without in this remote part of Mexico—was an eyebrow pencil.

"An eyebrow pencil?"

"You don't have a spare, do you?" she asked. "I know it would be the wrong color. You have such beautiful brown hair. But anything would help."

"No, Dottie. I don't use much makeup." None, in fact, on this trip.

Dottie was full of entirely unjustified optimism. She believed my Spanish was adequate to the job of finding a store in this remote spot that sold eyebrow pencils.

I didn't want to let her down.

"Okay, Dottie," I said. "Let's see what we can find." Aside from the train stop and the hotel, there were only a few simple houses in view.

The young woman in the lobby directed us to go through the courtyard past all the rooms and head up a dirt road to the store. She said we couldn't miss it.

Of course, we did. Several times, in fact, as we walked up and down the dirt road.

We said "buenos días" to a lot of people, and they cheerfully responded, even though it was afternoon and we were wishing them good morning. Spanish was the second language among these Tarahumara people, too, so they had reason to be particularly forgiving of our linguistic challenges. We smiled. They smiled. But nobody seemed to understand when I asked for the store.

Then we saw somebody come out of a tiny, unpainted building carrying a bag. The door was open. Inside was a counter. Behind it was a young woman. I greeted her and considered it a lucky break when she responded in Spanish. Dottie kept up a running commentary in English on how quaint the store was, how nice and attractive the woman behind the counter was, and how much she wished she hadn't lost her luggage. She punctuated it with enough laughter to get the young woman on her side. It was not hard to like Dottie. Her intentions were so unmistakably friendly.

I said we needed a *lapiz*—I knew that meant pencil—for . . . Well, I didn't know how to say eyebrow, so I did a little pantomime. The young woman said something I didn't understand and Dottie continued talking.

"Sweetheart," Dottie said to me, "tell her she's just so beautiful—¡*Muy bonita!*" she said loudly directly to the woman. "Tell her I just love her little store and I bet she's got a wonderful family and I'd just love to meet them. . . ."

I smiled and did my pantomime again. The young woman looked perplexed. Dottie kept talking. I tried again. Then the young woman smiled with sudden understanding and reached under the counter. She put a couple of eyebrow pencils on the counter in front of us.

I would have been only slightly less surprised if she'd produced Russian caviar or a copy of the Declaration of Independence. Dottie was beside herself with delight. This store not only had eyebrow pencils, it had one the right color for a gray-haired American lady.

Dottie needed a little good luck, and maybe all the smiles and goodwill of the Tarahumara people we met while looking for the store manifested itself in the Miracle of the Eyebrow Pencils.

It's an unlikely story. But it's true. I was there. And maybe that magic followed us back to the hotel and helped change my own luck.

It didn't happen with much drama. No birds burst into song when I first saw him. No rainbow appeared in the late-afternoon sky. There was just the clean smell of that canyon country mixed with the tang of cooking fires from the village. It was the golden hour just before sunset as Dottie and I crossed the hotel courtyard. She was talking about margaritas. I was hoping for some quiet time alone before dinner. As we entered the lobby, I saw Sixto for the first time. It was so undramatic that he still says he doesn't remember seeing me that day.

But I remember.

He was talking to our guide. She wanted him to take one of the women in our group on a short hike into the canyon to see some of the caves where the Tarahumara lived. Our guide asked if I wanted to go along. I said no and went to my room.

Sixto twisted his ankle on that hike. Because of the injury, he rode the train with us the next afternoon. He was training to be a manager for the family-owned hotel chain that included Posada Barrancas, the Santa Anita in Los Mochis, and the Hotel Misión in Cerocahui, where we would stay that night on our way back to Los Mochis, where Sixto would get his ankle looked at.

Our guide told us Cerocahui was for lovers. It certainly was not for the faint of heart.

The train stop was at the bottom of a big, steep hill. The hotel was at the top. A bus shuttled us up a cratered road of hairpin curves that gave those of us on the cliff side an unobstructed view of the canyon. Too unobstructed. As we wound our way up, my mother and I exchanged amazed looks at the nearness of the edge of the road, the depth of the drop-off, and the driver's speed.

Dottie simply gasped in pain. She needed a hip replacement, but resisted out of fear that the operation would leave her in a wheelchair. The jarring of the journey was agony for her. Sixto was sitting next to her, helping her brace against the worst of the bumps. She kept calling him "sweetie" and "señor" and telling him "thank you, gracias" over and over. During the few smooth places in that bumpy forty-minute ride, he would distract her with things like a pantomime in which he pretended to sew his fingers together. I wondered why he took such an interest in an elderly lady tourist. He didn't look like an opportunist.

The hotel was at the top of the world, but thankfully on level ground. Directly across the street was a stone mission built by the Jesuits three hundred years ago. It had a bell tower and an open front door. My mother and I checked out the dusky, cool interior while our guide and the bus driver got the luggage into the hotel. The eyes of the statues glistened and followed you as you moved around the sanctuary.

We walked back to the hotel and into what felt like the set of an old-time Pedro Infante movie about a beautiful girl who falls in love with the handsome vaquero that her rancher-father can't stand. My mother went to find Dottie, and I went to check out my room.

The thump of my purse on the dresser made me realize how quiet this place was. That rustic wooden dresser had an oil lamp and a sign that said the management sometimes turned off the electric generator at night. There was also a glass pitcher of ice water with clear plastic wrap stretched over the top. The person who put that pitcher there not only knew I was coming, she had also timed the placement of the water so the ice hadn't melted yet. There were flowers on the dresser, too. Fresh flowers. It was all enormously welcoming.

I showered off the dust from the bus ride and joined the others in the dining room. Our itinerary promised mariachis. But all I saw were a couple of kids in ranch clothes holding guitars and trying to disappear into the wall. Our tour guide set up some bar stools across from the communal dining table and motioned them over. They sat and tuned their guitars for a very long time, shooting glances at the door like they were measuring their chances for a quick escape.

Sixto entered the lobby, his ankle apparently not giving him much trouble, and our guide instantly propelled him toward the musicians and pulled up a chair for him. He didn't have a guitar, but the uncomfortable look on his face definitely made him look like part of the group. They could have called themselves the Reluctant Musicians or, if their wishes came true, the Escapees.

We watched them from a long wooden table where we were all being served a feast of tortilla soup, *carne asada*, fried potatoes, refried beans, homemade tortillas, and *salsa fresca*. This was followed by a dessert of flan that was as thick and pure as the cook's maiden sister.

Our guide kept a green glass pitcher of margaritas freshened up and circulating. I was drinking bottled water, though, which made me a spectator of the increasingly animated antics of the group that was lapping up the tequila. After the second pitcher, hardly anybody cared that the "mariachis" hadn't started singing. Members of our group were reenacting the robbery—with translation by our guide—for the two new people who had joined us on the train from Posada Barrancas.

Among the newcomers was an older American man who walked with a limp and wore sorrow and anger like a heavy cloak. His somewhat disinterested companion was a young Mexican woman who was dressed very casually.

She lit a cigarette and walked over to join the Reluctant Musicians. One of the young men gave her his seat and pulled up another stool. She took a deep drag on her cigarette, threw back her head, and blew a stream of smoke at the ceiling. Then she began singing "*Cielito Lindo*." The young men began strumming madly. She kept stroking Sixto's shoulder to get him to sing along. He might have uttered a word or two as he tried to shake off her hand—it was hard to tell.

When it was time for the *ay, ay, ay, ay* yodeling part, she thrust her cigarette at Sixto so she could really cut loose. He stopped singing instantly, and stared at the nasty thing she'd put in his hand. A sewer roach would have been more welcome. He held that cigarette at arm's length between the very tips of his thumb and first finger. His disgust was the strongest thing in the room.

As the song petered out, he thrust the burning cigarette back at her and left the area like a righteous man fleeing an expected bolt of lightning.

The live entertainment was over.

Our guide produced a boom box and the dancing began. I moved across the room to a massive couch with a good view. Sixto joined me.

His English was little better than my Spanish. But he tried. He asked my name. Then he asked me if I knew what my name meant in his language. I'd heard this line plenty of times before. But when Sixto said, "You are like your name," it did not sound like a line. He did not seem like the kind of man who knew many pickup lines.

We worked at having a conversation as the music and merriment of the dancers got louder. Our topic was the Bible. I said the original meaning can get distorted in translation. He agreed enthusiastically. I didn't know at the time that he'd spent many years studying the Bible and comparing what it said with what the Mennonite missionaries told him it meant.

Our conversation had a lot of white space, but the silences were not uncomfortable. We used them to watch the drama unfolding across the room.

The woman who had tried to sing "Cielito Lindo" was becoming increasingly rude to her companion. That had been noticed and overlooked by the rest of the party during dinner. But she was now becoming sexually provocative with one of the young guitar players. This was harder to overlook, especially since her companion was getting agitated. The young musician had refused to dance with the woman, but she didn't quit. Now she had him backed up against the kitchen door. Her companion tripped as he tried to lunge at her, then came up swinging when the young musician caught him. He was drunk and angry. She waved off his demands to return to their room and turned her attentions back to the young man.

Our guide huddled with a handsome, white-haired Mexican man who met us at the hotel when we arrived. He was our host, and a great dancer who'd been swinging my mother around the floor most of the evening. Now he nodded in agreement with our guide, who suddenly turned off the music and announced—a little too loudly—that the electricity would be going off in five minutes.

We all had to rush to our rooms and light our oil lamps, she said.

Like many of our guide's pronouncements, this one didn't hold up under scrutiny. After all, why not just light the oil lamps in the lobby? The boom box ran on batteries. But like all of our guide's pronouncements, this one was delivered with such an air of authority that nobody questioned her.

She told us not to waste time. On this moonless night in a village small enough to fit at the sharp edge of a canyon ridge, finding the matches and getting the lamps lit would be a lot easier before the lights went out.

The others started moving toward the door.

Then our guide came over, put one hand on my shoulder and the other on Sixto's. Not to worry, she whispered, the story about the lights was just a ruse to get the woman—she called her a prostitute—to go back to the room with the old man who'd hired her. The lights would go out, our guide said, but the party would continue in a private room that had its own generator. We were to pretend to go to bed, then follow the path around to the back of the hotel to meet her for the after-party. Plenty of margaritas, she promised, though neither I nor Sixto were drinking. She scurried off to clue in the rest of our group.

Everybody made a lot of good-night noises and milled around in the patio until the woman reluctantly entered their room with her escort and shut the door. Then we started down the path and entered a room next to a sign that said, "En vino veritas."

The group was a lot smaller. It was already late and some people, including my mother, decided to use the last of the electricity to light their lamps and get ready for bed. Our guide was there, of course, with another full pitcher of margaritas. Dottie was ready for more partying, as were the other members of the reluctant mariachi band. They filled up their glasses with margaritas. Sixto declined. He clearly found the alcohol as distressing as that cigarette.

I had brought a glass of water. I held it out to him. He asked what it was, and just to be sure, smelled it carefully before he took a drink. I was more amused than insulted. I'd never seen anyone so unsettled by cigarettes and alcohol.

The spirit of the party was fully broken. This room had none of the charm of the main hotel. It was small and full of cheap modern furniture instead of all that massive old wooden stuff. There were no quaint Mexican pots or tin-framed mirrors on the walls. This was a room for serious drinking. Sixto was sitting on the other side of a laminated cocktail table. We passed the water glass back and forth as the rest of the group finished the pitcher and told jokes I couldn't understand and Sixto didn't seem to enjoy. Before long, Dottie asked me to help her find her room. When I rose, she asked Sixto to come along and help me find mine.

I could see the twinkle in her eye, even in that light.

It was womb dark as we made our way down the path and onto the thick, damp grass of the courtyard patio. Dottie gave Sixto her key and I waited while he found her room and lit the oil lamp for her. After he left her and shut the door, the night was so quiet it made my ears hum. The stars jostled each other for space in the crowded sky. Some of them lost their place and fell with a big show into the blackness. I'd never seen such a busy night sky.

When Sixto rejoined me, I expected him to try to kiss me. It's what an American man would have done in this situation. Instead, he just stood at a respectful distance as we looked up at the amazing celestial display. His attitude during the evening demonstrated that he was attracted to me, so his behavior was a little baffling.

Then he asked which room was mine. Oh, I thought, now he'll make his move.

I hadn't decided how I would respond. But he didn't give me a choice.

He unlocked the door, used his last match to light my lamp. Then he left.

The next morning he was waiting in the courtyard outside my room. He invited me to walk around before breakfast.

We toured the village and I took pictures, and I never thought to ask about his ankle. He seemed fine. Then we went into the old mission. The statues inside were as elegant as they'd been the day before, when I saw them with my mother. They watched us cross into the baptistery. I followed Sixto up an old wooden ladder into the bell tower. It felt a little like a dream as he helped me pull myself up from the last rung—which didn't quite reach the floor of the bell tower. I've never been comfortable with ladders or heights. But suddenly, there I was, looking out an open arch over a village that had been founded by missionaries in 1694, and well used by its residents ever since.

Sixto started singing to me as we sat there.

I didn't understand the words. He told me much later that the song was about Jesus restoring life to the dried old bones of sinners. At the time, I didn't care about the words. His voice was clear and fine. No wonder our guide thought he should be part of last night's singing group. But this performance was heartfelt, not tense and shrouded by some sinner's cigarette smoke. When he was done, he put on my *Arizona Daily Star* hat and I took a picture of him sitting in the arched opening of the bell tower.

I was in love.

We sat together on the train ride back to Los Mochis and laughed most of the way. When we got to the Santa Anita, Sixto asked me to have dinner with him. I took a shower, changed, and met him in the lobby. We walked to a small restaurant where I was the only non-Mexican. He spent a lot of time asking the waiter about whether the water was purified and assuring me that he knew the kitchen was clean.

After dinner, we took a walk that was right out of my worst nightmare.

The sun was gone and so were the bright colors. There was just enough light left to see that the sidewalks of Mochis were literally crawling with sewer roaches. Usually, this would have sent me screaming for the hotel, which could be relied on to be clean and insect free.

But I didn't run. Neither did Sixto. We held hands and stomped our feet with every step to keep the roaches from running up our legs. He said he'd never seen anything like this. I never wanted to see it again. Yet we kept stomp-walking as the big, feces-colored bugs swarmed across the street and sidewalk. Some were linked together by their back ends and I thought, my God, if this is roach sex, I really don't need to see it.

We made our way to a beautiful plaza. This is where we should have been able to linger and talk. But we couldn't stop. The roaches were swarming under the dragon-headed cast-iron light posts. Sitting on a bench was out of the question. We had to keep moving and stomping to clear a path.

I have been to Mochis many times since, and thankfully, have never seen a repeat performance. That night was my "Beauty and the Beast" moment. No matter how ugly things got, I didn't let go of Sixto's hand. We tap-danced around those horrible creatures to keep the evening from ending.

Back at the hotel, the sidewalk was clear of bugs—as I knew it would be. We crossed into the lavishly furnished lobby. He rode up in the elevator with me and opened the door of my room. I entered. He stood at the threshold. We exchanged two brief kisses and he said good night. Our time was up.

In the morning, our group was leaving.

He came to say goodbye over breakfast, as gracious to Dottie, my mother, and our guide as he was to me. I gave him two of my business cards. On one, he wrote his name and the name of the village nearest to the ejido where his mother lived. He said he could get mail there, but it was iffy. He gave this card back to me. He kept the other one. I didn't really expect to see him again. But I didn't feel the same kind of sad I would have felt a week earlier.

Somewhere between the Mystery of the Open Doors, the Miracle of the Eyebrow Pencil, and the Plague of Roaches, I'd been transformed. I felt good. Mexico had been transformed in my mind, too, from the simple to the complex.

Wary of the bus, our guide had hired a van to take us back to the border. She either forgot to ask about the air-conditioning or she'd been misinformed. Either way, nothing happened when we asked the driver to turn it on. It was hot, and there were arguments about how far to leave the windows open and who got to sit next to them. We were no longer such a merry band of travelers. We stopped for lunch at a nice seafood restaurant in Hermosillo. During the meal, one of the men in our group yelled out "Hey, José! Bring me a beer." His wife shushed him.

"How do you know his name is José?" she asked.

"When you want a beer, they're all named *José*," he said, snapping his fingers at the waiter.

I thought of Sixto, trying to distract Dottie as she winced in pain on the bus ride to the Hotel Misión. I thought of him walking us to our rooms in the dark.

As we stood at the cash register to pay our separate checks, this same guy gave me a lecherous look and said, "I guess you had fun."

I thought of those two kisses in the doorway of my hotel room the night before. Because I had not "had fun" in the sense he meant, I wasn't susceptible to his attempt to make me feel dirty. So I just looked at him. His twin images of Mexican men went from José bringing cerveza to gigolos bringing a good time to traveling American women. The range was much narrower than those female icons our bus driver had displayed on his dashboard. There was no benevolent spirit in his vision of Mexican men. Yet this American tourist and that Mexican bus driver shared a similar myopia.

CHAPTER THREE

People said I was softer when I got back. Not as tightly wound. Not as angry. I cleaned up my language, and that was quite a loss for those who appreciate creative profanity. I started going to church and I began exploring hiking clubs, spent more time working out, and went on a diet regime that included lots of greens and no sugar or white flour. When my ex-boyfriend decided it was time to get back together, I turned him down.

I showed everybody the picture of Sixto in the bell tower.

I composed a letter to Sixto telling him that I would help him if he ever wanted to come to the United States. I said he was too good, too talented, to spend his life catering to tourists. I don't know if anybody ever got that letter. I know he didn't.

About a month after I got back from Mexico, I was returning from a workout in the newspaper's employee gym when I heard one of my coworkers take a call on my line.

"She works here," she said in Spanish, "but she doesn't speak Spanish. Maybe I can help you."

I knew instantly. It was Sixto. He was in Nogales, on the Mexican side.

I banged my hip on the corner of my desk rushing to get to the phone. When I heard his voice, I felt a rush of heat flash up my body. Too bad I couldn't really understand what he was saying. After enough repetition, I got this much: He was at *"la linea."* On the Mexican side. I told him I'd be there as soon as I could.

I left right after work and began a ritual that I would repeat twice a week for six weeks. First there was the hour-and-a-half drive from Tucson to the border. I would speed all the way in my dark blue Toyota Tercel. I parked at a Safeway just this side of the line. It's gone now, but in those days, it did great business with residents from the Mexican side who would slip through holes to shop American style. They returned to Mexico with plastic grocery bags hanging from both arms. Now the Border Patrol looks you over as you leave, and on the Mexican side you are required to push a button that will randomly determine whether the Mexican customs officials question you about what you are bringing into their country. If the light turns red when you push the button, they stop you. If it's green, you go on your way.

Back in 1988, you just walked through a big turnstile and you were there.

And "there" was definitely a challenging place for a young woman who'd gotten all dressed up to impress a man. As I crossed the line, I remembered the voice of an old family friend who had taken my sister and me to Mexico when I was fifteen years old.

"Say goodbye," he told us as we drove across the line in his Cadillac. "You just left all of your constitutional rights behind."

Now, I emerged into a kind of no-man's land between the border fence and the bustling city of Nogales, Sonora, to look for Sixto. It was the first time I'd crossed the border alone. It wasn't just my constitutional rights I'd left behind. I suddenly lacked any sense of what to do or how to act. I lingered uncomfortably in that transition zone between two worlds. Most people moved quickly toward the border inspection station or back home with their bags of groceries. But there were men who inhabited that in-between space—taxi drivers looking for fares and predators looking for aimless people like me. I tried to scan the area without looking like I was looking for someone. I didn't see Sixto. I felt very vulnerable, so I started back across the border. Safely within the threshold of the US inspection station, I turned around for one last look. There he was, rushing toward me.

"I thought you were leaving," he said.

He was dressed in black polyester pants with a yellow shirt. His hair, which he cut himself, looked coarse and ragged. We held hands as we walked to the plaza behind a big Catholic church. There were cast-iron benches that had been painted white some time ago, and a big gazebo, where kids ran up and down the stairs as their mothers gossiped in little groups. Vendors sold plastic cups of cut-up fruit or peanuts soaking in chili sauce. There were sounds of bicycle bells, church bells, and the low growl of old, old buses lined up on one side of the plaza. Kids in blue-and-white school uniforms swarmed out of the buses. Women with armloads of groceries hurried on board. Old men pulled themselves up the stairs by the railing just before the bus driver leaned down to pull the door shut and drive off. As soon as one left, another bus quickly pulled into the empty space.

On the other side of the plaza, against the walls of storefronts that sold baked goods or music tapes, there were dark women in ragged, faded clothes—indigenous people from the south of Mexico, Sixto explained. They sat with babies wrapped up in shawls and begged from passers-by with hands outstretched, sometimes touching the legs of those who rushed on down the street. Their children—little boys and girls who would have been in kindergarten if they'd been born two miles north—wandered around the plaza trying to sell packets of chicle from small cardboard boxes that they held in front of them and thrust up at you with imploring looks.

Sixto and I would sit, side by side, on those iron benches for hours. We used our limited language skills as best we could, but mostly we looked into each other's eyes and saw the future.

It was summer, but the dark still came too soon. We held hands as he walked me back to the border. Then we'd kiss goodbye, and I'd return to a world where I understood the language and knew the rules. He'd wait until I passed the inspection and emerged on the other side, as though he could do something if I ran into trouble. Sometimes I could see him, and we'd wave. But usually all I could see when I looked back was a crowd of strangers.

We did this twice a week for six weeks.

Early on, we were determined that he would cross the border legally. I was an educated person. A journalist. I figured I could use the system. I called the Immigration and Naturalization Service. They told me he'd need to take an affidavit of support from me to the American Embassy in Hermosillo. But first, Sixto had to get a passport from Mexico onto which the visa would be attached. This required several trips to various offices and a number of bribes. That's how things are done in Mexico. We fulfilled the requirements and he got the passport.

Then it was my turn. I filled out the affidavit of support, swearing I was prepared to provide for his support, if necessary, so that he would never go on welfare or cost the US taxpayer any money. In order to demonstrate my ability to do this, I had to get my boss to write a letter saying I had a permanent job. This required some persuasion.

"No job is permanent," he told me. He said I could use such a letter in court if they ever tried to lay me off.

"It just means permanent as opposed to temporary," I said. "It doesn't mean I can never be fired."

"I can't sign something that says your job is permanent," he said. "No job is permanent."

I was doomed.

I cajoled. He thought about it. Eventually, he signed the letter.

I had everything my government told me I needed. That meant we were set.

On the American side of the line, I thought smugly, things worked without bribes. We had a straightforward legal process. Follow the rules, complete the requirements, and you get the desired result. I gave Sixto the papers, and he took the bus to Hermosillo to visit the US Embassy. They turned him down flat. No explanation. No guidance on what to do next.

The system didn't work.

US immigration officials I'd talked to on the phone hadn't told me that it didn't matter how carefully I filled out the forms, or how successfully I convinced my boss to go out on a limb for me—the request for a visa would be denied.

After the first denial, we tried again with all new papers. He made several trips to the US Embassy. He carried with him the broomstick of the Witch of the North. But the wizards wouldn't budge. They just said no.

No. No.

Meanwhile, tens of thousands of people were using holes in

the fence.

You could watch it happen from the windows of the old Mc-Donald's in downtown Nogales, Arizona. Any one of a dozen tables offered a long view of the fence that divided Arizona from Sonora. It was simple mesh fence then, and it had dozens of holes. Half a dozen people crossed in the time it took to eat a cheeseburger. You could see them duck through a hole, dash across a grass-covered hill on the US side, and disappear into a neighborhood on the outskirts of town. There were holes leading to downtown Nogales, too. These led into business districts. Not everybody who entered illegally planned to stay in the United States. People went both ways through those holes. Some shopped. Some came across to visit family and then went home. Some of them even had visas, but found it easier to avoid the lines and cross at more convenient locations.

The fear, the intense suspicion, the violence that surrounds the border today was just a distant cloud on the horizon of twin communities that were intertwined and interdependent.

We hadn't wanted to break the law—even if it was a law that seemed very loosely enforced. By now, though, it was obvious the system was not going to work for us. So now we did talk about breaking the law.

The barrier was the border. Once that was overcome, nobody cared who was in the country illegally. It was a policy of hypocrisy that included a danger zone in Arizona that lay between Nogales and Tucson. If I were caught with Sixto in my car along that stretch of highway, the government could seize my vehicle—the feds had made a great show of doing just that to intimidate church groups that were offering sanctuary to Central American refugees. If caught, I might lose my job, too.

Sixto didn't want me to take the risk. He still wanted to come legally.

So our time sitting in the plaza became melancholy.

We took a walk around the city as if movement of any kind would help. Our conversation reinforced our gloom. Sixto needed a job, and Nogales offered few options. He started thinking about heading back to Los Mochis to resume his career at the hotel. He said he could keep trying to get a visa from there. But we both knew that wouldn't work any better than what we'd been trying. There would be no visa.

After he left, there would be no more days together in the plaza, either.

It would be over.

Our walk took us to a cemetery. It was a messy but inexplicably optimistic place.

Paths zigzagged between gravestones that were scattered about helter-skelter. Some were carved granite, with elegant script attempting to immortalize a name and a lifespan. Others were cast concrete with lumpy lambs or angels perched on top. There were ornate wrought-iron markers and weathered wooden ones. Tumbledown picket fences hung limply around some graves. Other graves were heaped with plastic flowers and surrounded by proud, brightly painted pickets. There were withered once-live flowers, too. And paper flowers in various shades of fading colors. And candles—those still burning at the bottom of deep glass cylinders and those that had burned out long ago, like the lives they commemorated.

This was not a sad place or a defeated place. It was more about the living than the dead. It had a sense of humor. It poked death in the eye.

Sixto took my hand as I pointed to an interesting plant that was flowering at the side of a cross-shaped stone marker. I looked at our hands. Mine looked very light in his. I wondered aloud what color skin our children might have. Then we kissed among all those gravestones. It was the kind of kiss lovers exchange before they've gotten used to each other. Hungry.

I drove home in the dark that night with the sense of resignation one gets from the uniform and orderly markers of US cemeteries. We'd done all we could. Our dreams would have to live on in a better place, because this world was not going to accommodate them.

I could not make a living in his country. My government refused to let him enter mine. It was an impasse. A Mexican standoff. There was nothing more I could do.

But that didn't mean there was nothing more that could be done.

Sixto was staying at a church in Nogales, Sonora, that took in migrants. These men got a place to sleep and home-cooked meals in exchange for listening to fiery Gospel lessons and doing chores. Both of these requirements were easy for Sixto. He was used to working hard. What's more, his Bible was one of the few things he'd tucked into the satchel he brought from Mochis. He could talk for hours about the Bible with just about anyone.

Most of the men staying at the church were either waiting to jump the line or deciding whether to try again after being sent back by the border patrol. These were the days before the rise of criminal smugglers known as coyotes, whose services became necessary as the United States hardened the border. Coyotes charge a fee for safe passage through the border gauntlet to jobs in the United States. As the border got more difficult to cross, the fees went up, and criminal syndicates took over. Today's coyotes work for cartels. They take migrants on dangerous treks through the brutal desert and often leave them to die in the 120-degree heat. Migrants are raped, robbed, or held for ransom in drop houses in Phoenix. They keep coming because they can still get jobs.

But in those days, you didn't have to hire help to cross the line. You just stepped through the hole. The border patrol couldn't watch all the holes, so many people made it through. Those who got caught were returned to Mexico in time to try again before sunset. Many of the guys at that Assembly of God Church where Sixto was staying had done that. They laughed when he made his trips to Hermosillo to try for a visa. They knew he wouldn't get it. But they liked him because he was always upbeat and interested in their lives and challenges. He knew scripture, too, and they respected that.

After our walk in the cemetery, though, Sixto moped around the church. He didn't laugh anymore. He didn't care about what their wives said when they borrowed the preacher's phone and called home. He didn't sit and tell Bible stories after dinner anymore. One of the men announced that he was sick of seeing Sixto look so miserable.

"*Ven*," he said. Come.

He led Sixto to a hole in the border fence and went through.

Sixto followed him. That was it.

Years later, we went back to take a picture of that hole and put it in the family album.

The mesh fence was replaced with a solid fence made of steel landing mats, which became a patchwork of holes that were cut on the Mexican side and welded shut on the American side. Then the US government decided to spend some more tax dollars replacing the landing mats with a see-through barrier of bollards. Now the criminal smugglers use different routes and dig tunnels. But like I said, in those days, things were different.

Sixto entered the United States near downtown. As soon as he crossed, he quickly blended into the crowd of pedestrians in that largely Latino community. Once he was a few blocks from the border, there was little likelihood he would be challenged. But there remained the journey to Tucson. Along that road, the border patrol did have checkpoints, and they did challenge those heading north. He didn't call me. But he had a plan.

That night, Sixto slept in the bushes in front of a Catholic Church not far from the border. Maybe that's where he picked up the Twin Miracles of the Unexamined Passport and the Unasked Question. These were the two things he needed.

The next morning, he bought a bus ticket to Tucson. When the border patrol stopped the bus to check people's papers, Sixto simply handed the agent his Mexican passport. The agent looked at the picture, looked at Sixto, and handed back the passport without checking for a visa. That was the first miracle. The agent didn't ask anything. That was the second miracle. It meant Sixto didn't have to lie. To this day my husband cannot tell a believable lie—even about whether he likes what I give him for Christmas. From then on, all he had to do was leave the driving to Greyhound.

He called me at work when he arrived in Tucson.

I went to pick him up at a plaza that was very different from the one where we had spent so many hours. Tucson's El Presidio Park is on the site of a 1775 Spanish presidio. But there is little sense of history and less life. The walkways are new and swept clean. There are no cast-iron benches with misty-eyed lovers, no vendors, no old men on bicycles, no rows of buses, no women rushing to climb aboard with armloads of groceries. There weren't very many beggars, either. Not in the summer. The beggars in this city are called the homeless, and they leave for cooler locations in late spring. No wonder.

The plaza was suffocating as the sun reflected white-hot off the concrete surfaces all around; even the pigeons had found someplace shady to wait out the heat.

The place looked empty when I arrived.

I thought maybe I had misunderstood when he explained where he was. If so, I'd have to go back to the paper and wait for him to call again. I had no way to contact him, and this was before cell phones.

As I looked around, I could feel my clothes wilting in the heat. My bangs were starting to stick to my forehead.

Then I saw him step from behind a wall where he'd been waiting. Not hiding, exactly. But not wanting to stand out as the only living thing in that blazing plaza, either. It was the first time I had ever seen him when he wasn't surrounded by the bustle of Mexico, the colors, the noise, the people. He didn't look foreign. Not exactly. But still. Anyone would be able to see that he'd stepped out of another world.

He was walking toward me.

Now what?

I had envisioned this moment as a time of squealing for joy and dancing around with hugs and laughter. Instead, I moved quietly so I wouldn't wake up. If this was real—if I was awake—then our faith and our commitment to be together had been realized. But there are few places more surreal than a concrete-clad downtown Tucson plaza in the midday summer heat. So it might not be real.

We walked toward each other with a demeanor more suited for church than a celebration. This was scary. We both knew the border was only the first barrier we were going to have to overcome. He was a poor man from a developing country, and he had few skills that would be applicable in my world. My understanding of his world and culture didn't go much beyond writing cautionary editorials about the dangers of drinking too much on Cinco de Mayo.

I was the child of middle-class America. I grew up believing poverty was a kind of illness that people got from being lazy enough to get born on the wrong side of town. As for Sixto, he'd learned about my culture from missionaries, tourists, and an occasional Abbott and Costello movie shown on a bedsheet hung up in a lot next to his mother's house. This was probably the first plaza he'd ever seen that was utterly empty of people. I might have used a *Twilight Zone* analogy to describe the feeling that all the people had just vanished. But he would not have understood.

He had no idea what *Twilight Zone* was.

We didn't embrace. We didn't shout. We didn't jump up and down. We held hands as we walked to my car.

I drove him to my duplex and opened the door on amenities that I took for granted. Cool air. Indoor plumbing. Telephone. Television. Tape player. Radios. Electric stove. Microwave. A big refrigerator, where I kept the barbeque chicken that I told him he could eat for lunch. Seven fully tiled rooms with carpet under the couch. He knew these things from the hotels and maybe the houses of the missionaries. Never in his mother's home. Never among his contemporaries. But he didn't exclaim or act surprised. Like the plaza, this was another fixed-up place that was empty of people. I lived alone in a space big enough for several families.

When I left to go back to work, he asked if he should wait outside until I returned. I said no, he should make himself at home.

As I drove away, I wondered what I was doing. He was a stranger really. A man I'd known for a little over two months, most of it spent trying to communicate in a boisterous border-town plaza. Now I'd given him the key to my home and access to everything I'd worked to achieve. I had no idea what this was going to mean.

"When the dream came, I held my breath with my eyes closed."   That line from the Buffalo Springfield song went through my head.

The dream had arrived. He was in my house.

What now?

Back at work, I deflected questions, finished my writing, and waited for the clock to release me.

When I got home, he was waiting outside. He'd locked the door on the way out—on purpose. He was smiling the same way he used to smile when we spotted each other after I crossed the border.

When I unlocked the door, everything looked the same—only everything was different. The house didn't feel empty anymore. He'd tidied up a few things. He had also eaten one piece of chicken before washing the plate—along with the other dishes I'd left in the sink that morning.

The awkwardness of earlier was gone now. This time we did embrace. We kissed for a very long time. I felt complete and happy in his arms.

But we didn't do more than kiss and stroke each other's hair and share the tender touches that are about promise, not fulfillment.

Later that evening, my mother brought over a single-bed mattress, which we put in the second bedroom. During the days, we spent a lot of time kissing and cuddling. But every night he slept on that mattress. He did not want to dishonor our love with premarital sex.

CHAPTER FOUR

Two weeks later, we were married by a justice of the peace at the old courthouse that opens onto El Presidio Park. I didn't tell anyone before we did it because I didn't want to hear all the reasons why I shouldn't do it. I couldn't have countered those arguments. I couldn't have argued that what I was about to do made sense. It didn't. But I knew it was the right thing to do, just as surely as I knew that nobody would understand that.

The judge's secretary said she could be a witness, but we'd need somebody else. So we asked a woman waiting in the hallway if she'd help us out. She was thrilled to do it. We said our vows in the judge's chambers, between cases. Later, after Sixto earned enough money, we bought real wedding rings. But that day, I gave him one I was wearing on my right hand so he could put it on my left at the appropriate time in the ceremony.

We got married early Friday morning so we'd have the weekend at home together. But after the ceremony, we both went to work—he'd gotten a job at a travel agency that catered to Mexican travelers.

That evening, we joined my mother and Dottie at the VFW club. On a trip to the restroom, I told my mother we'd just gotten married. When she realized I wasn't joking, she looked stunned. "What are you going to live on?" she asked. It was a pretty silly question, really, because I had a good job and had been living on my own for some time.

"On love," I answered. It was a pretty silly answer.

I had just legally given away half of everything I owned and earned to a man who arrived in the country with only the clothes on his back. My mother's reaction was more realistic than mine.

But I was operating on pure emotion. And it felt good.

When we got back to the table and told Dottie, she squealed with delight and hugged us over and over. She regaled us with stories about her "Mexican husband," and urged me to translate everything she said for Sixto, which, of course, I couldn't do.

In those early days, all we wanted was to be alone together, and when we weren't alone together we were thinking about being alone together. We kept the Spanish-English dictionary handy for the times when words were necessary. Most translations went from Spanish into English. Sixto wanted to learn English, so we spoke English. He enrolled in an English as a Second Language class at the community college.

Sixto has a natural grace and elegance. He looks elegant in whatever he wears. But all he had to wear when he arrived was one pair of pants and two shirts. One of the first things we did was go to a secondhand store to get him some clothes. It was the Disabled American Veterans Store on Twenty-Second Street, long gone now, but then one of my mother's favorites. She knew all the best secondhand stores in town. This place delivered the Miracle of the Right-sized Clothes. We both decided that God must have seen us coming, because we never again found such a quality selection in his size. He wore size twenty-nine pants in those days, but his shoulders were broad. On that trip, we outfitted him nicely for very little money.

We attributed a lot of things to God or miracles or magic in those days. That's how it felt. The world sparkled. Life was a series of happy surprises. We laughed. We made love. We took walks to places that seemed far more interesting than they had ever seemed before.

He also worked.

That first job at the travel agency involved running errands in a car that had expired plates and no insurance. Sixto had no driver's license, either. His boss paid him five dollars a day. I was outraged, but he was okay with it. He didn't want to sit around all day, and he wasn't cut out for any of the typical undocumented-worker jobs. I was middle-class, after all, and we had standards. So I would drop him off at her office on my way to work and pick him up at the end of the day. He finished every day smelling of her cigarette smoke.

This woman thought she was doing us a great favor one day when she sent him home with a box from the food bank. Apparently she had gotten herself certified to distribute food to the poor in her area. I was deeply offended at being offered food that should have gone to people who really needed it. But I had to keep my outrage in check while I explained the concept of a food bank to Sixto. Then I had to explain that the woman he worked for was apparently scamming the system. He was offended then, too. And embarrassed. He never brought home another box of food.

We thought his prospects were improving when another woman—also Spanish speaking—hired him to go door-to-door and do surveys for some sort of marketing outfit. It would have paid better. Much better. If she'd ever paid him. But there was always some excuse. After several weeks, I went in and confronted her. She kept looking at him and trying to ignore me. I told her what she was doing was against the law. She paid him then. But said she never wanted to see either of us again. He went back to the travel agency and got a small raise.

I spent a lot of time explaining things.

He couldn't understand why we had homeless people; he'd thought the United States was a rich country. He was surprised to see so many Mexican people; I had to tell him that they didn't like being called "Mexican." It was tough trying to make him understand that the name of people from his country had been turned into something of an insult in mine. Call them Mexican American or Latino or Hispanic, I said. He liked Latino better, because Hispanic carried too close a tie to a colonial power that had not been good for Mexico. His mother, he told me, had indigenous roots.

Sixto had left a bag behind at the church in Nogales, Sonora. After all, he hadn't understood that they'd be crawling through a hole in the fence when his friend took him for a walk the day he jumped the line. Once he was across, there was no question of going back. He didn't care much about the clothes in the bag. But he missed his Bible. A friend had given us a Spanish-English Bible as a postwedding gift, and we read it almost every day. But the one waiting at the church in Mexico was more than just a book of scripture. It had a handmade cover, well-worn pages, and carried the memories of years of study with family and friends.

When my mother heard about this, she offered to drive with me to Nogales to pick it up. On the way down, she and I discussed elaborate cloak-and-dagger stories to explain why we were bringing back a small bag of men's items and a Spanish-language Bible. But when we carried it back across the line, the US official just asked if we were US citizens. He didn't ask the usual second question: "What are you bringing back from Mexico?" That made things much easier.

My mother wasn't a good liar, either.

I think that's one reason she and Sixto hit it off right away. She could tell he made me happy, and, of course, that was a plus. But lots of the jerks I'd brought home to meet her over the years had made me happy—at least temporarily. She hadn't warmed up to them the way she did to Sixto. She told me it was his openness that she liked so much. He was without artifice or guile. His smile was instant, genuine, and contagious. He also valued family relationships, so he was eager to spend time at my mother's trailer.

The mesquite trees around her trailer have grown tall over the years because she planted vegetables under them, so they got lots of water. The wildflowers on her acre grew lush because she selectively pulled out the plants that weren't pretty or produced stickers that got caught in the long hair between her golden retriever's toes. She knew every tree and cactus on the place, and kept things pruned enough so they didn't run wild, but wild enough so it looked like a desert. She loved that land.

Sixto and I went out there almost every weekend, and he did chores for her. They had running jokes about the way the cacti seemed to have it in for him. She could—and did—work among the cacti all day and not get a sticker. Cactus spines gravitated to Sixto. She kept the tweezers handy as they worked together, hours at a time, often under the hot sun, pruning her mesquite trees, taking out mistletoe, moving rocks, pulling up the non-native grasses and other unwelcome plants that crowded out her wildflowers. She always kept Coke on hand for him. When they took a break, she'd make Coke floats with vanilla ice cream. They'd sit in the shade and sip their drinks. She didn't speak any Spanish, but they communicated just fine right from the beginning.

They were comfortable together. Kindred spirits. They both loved me unconditionally.

Sixto got his first taste of American holidays at her place on Thanksgiving. She always had a houseful of guests, and the food, of course, was terrific. My sister got married that same year we did, and her family—including her son from a previous marriage and her new husband's son—joined my mother's current boyfriend, along with Dottie and several neighbors, at a big portable table she set up in the living room.

The holiday was about family and food, so naturally, Sixto loved it.

It was his first traditional American turkey dinner, and he made my mother happy by piling his plate high and taking seconds of everything. He didn't drink the wine, but he didn't condemn it, either. If he was shocked at my sister's smoking, he never let on. Sixto talked to the kids about soccer and they became fast friends. This was his element.

From then on, he insisted that we get dressed up for all family get-togethers—even if it was just the three of us sitting in the backyard to watch fireworks on the Fourth of July. If a day was special enough to celebrate, a person ought to dress for it. Holidays became more formal affairs.

There was more hugging and kissing, too.

My mother and I had been through a lot together, and we were always close. But we hadn't done much hugging since I was a child—just perfunctory and somewhat self-conscious embraces when either of us was leaving on a trip or returning from one. That changed when Sixto entered the picture. He brought the Mexican custom of hello and goodbye embraces.

When my mother arrived at our place, he was opening the door to welcome her before she was out of the car. There was no pretense of being too cool or too busy. Enthusiastic embraces became a matter of course. It felt good, so it didn't take long to become habitual.

My mother introduced him to a man who did custodial work around her church, and he gave Sixto a real job with fair wages. No questions were asked about his immigration status. Nobody really cared then.

Except us. We cared. We began the paperwork to get him legal status.

CHAPTER FIVE

As his wife, I was able to petition to get Sixto a visa and permanent residency. But it wasn't automatic, and I knew from my attempts to get him a visa that there was probably a lot more to it than US immigration officials would take the time to explain over the phone. We went to Catholic Social Services, and paid a fee to have a caseworker shepherd us through the process. He was efficient and thorough.

He helped us fill out lots of forms. Then we waited.

After about five months—a remarkably fast response, our caseworker told us—we were given an appointment at the US Embassy in Tijuana. The letter came with a list of forms, pictures, and sworn statements we had to bring with us. It said if we missed the appointment for any reason or failed to bring the requested paperwork, we would not be eligible for another appointment for at least a year. Keeping the appointment meant we had to cross the border into Mexico. If they refused to give him the visa we were seeking, I'd be returning alone and he'd be stuck in Tijuana, which is a lot farther from Tucson than Nogales.

Before we went, we heard a lot of rumors about what the process was like. People told us we would have to strip naked and stand in lines—separated by gender, we hoped—for an examination. Somebody else told Sixto we would be taken into different offices and cross-examined to find out if our marriage was genuine or sham. My editor told me not to worry about that: You both glow when you are together, she said.

Somebody else told Sixto they would ask us about each other's favorite foods to see if we really lived together. We spent weeks quizzing each other on things we'd never thought about before. What was his favorite food? What was *mine*? I had no idea. Peaches? No. Steak? No. Strawberries? We decided his favorite colors were gray and maroon. Mine were black and red. We tried to think of everything. When we asked the careful man at Catholic Social Services about all the things people were saying, he told us to focus on getting the paperwork in order.

By the time we were ready, the stack of papers was an inch thick. We had sent letters to the police departments of every city in Mexico where Sixto had lived, and included their responses, which said he had never been in trouble with the law and was not wanted by the police. His mother sent his birth certificate, school records, and other family information. I worried about the Mexican mail system, but all the necessary papers arrived on time. Angels carried them. Also included in that packet for our trip to Tijuana were copies of our marriage certificate, my tax returns, notarized letters from my credit union and my employer, pictures of each of us taken professionally according to a detailed set of instructions, which included pulling our hair back off our ears and sitting at a particular angle. Painstakingly prepared forms were stacked in the right order. I put everything in a file and put the file in a manila envelope, which I planned to carry with me at all times. I also added some pictures from our Thanksgiving and from a baptism of a friend's daughter for whom we'd been asked to be godparents. I thought this would help prove we were really a couple. I tucked the appointment letter from the State Department into my purse. We were ready.

My mother drove us to the airport and we flew to San Diego. We took the train to the border and walked into Mexico. I held the manila envelope against my chest. One missing paper, one incorrectly filled-out form, and I'd be going home alone.

Our appointment at the embassy was at 8:00 a.m. Monday, April 17, 1989. The letter said we had to visit a particular doctor in Tijuana before then, so Sixto could get a blood test and chest X-ray. We had to do that on Friday, which meant we had to get to Tijuana Thursday and pay for four nights at the hotel. This would turn out to be just one example of my government's cavalier disinterest in our best interests.

The next morning, the taxi driver took us to the doctor's office and drove away. It was a quiet residential street. We checked the address on the letter, then knocked on the door. It wasn't a surprise that no one answered. The house looked as lonely as I was beginning to feel. We knocked again, hoping one of those angels that helped with the mail would pop up with a friendly doctor. But the door remained resolutely closed. The windows were blind. We kept knocking, because there was nothing else to do. Finally a woman stuck her head out of a second-story window of the house next door.

"*Se fueron al mar*," she yelled at us. They went to the ocean. The doctor wasn't coming back till next week.

So where would he get the blood test and chest X-ray? Who would give us the official form we needed to add to our packet for the Monday appointment?

The woman disappeared back into her house. We stood looking at each other.

The trees along the street were tall and still. The dappled shade on the pavement looked like permanent staining. As we walked back toward a main road, our shadows danced in and out of the dark places. We came to a small church and heard a Mass going on inside. Sixto said it would be a good place to sit down and think, so we entered the open door, pausing to let our eyes adjust to a deeper shade of shadow. There was the familiar smell of church candles and incense, which always make me think of what the nuns used to call the Mystery of Faith.

As we sat down, the priest was moving things around on the altar. He looked right at me and sneezed. He sneezed a few more times as he served Communion to a few old women in black rebozos. After each sneeze, he would glance at me as though I had brought something into the church that offended his nose. I was the only non-Mexican in the place. Sixto nodded toward the door and we went outside. By comparison, the shade-dappled street now looked bright, and we had to pause on the steps to let our eyes adjust.

I didn't feel so bad anymore; the priest made me laugh.

"Maybe he's allergic to *gringas*," I said.

Sixto was already moving toward a phone that was mounted on a pole in front of the church. He asked me to see if the appointment letter listed a number for the doctor's office.

"What good would that do," I said, as I felt for the letter. "He's not there."

But there was a number, and Sixto dialed it.

This became our Miracle of the Sneezing Priest: somebody answered. Sixto explained our situation. Then he waited. Then he explained again. And waited. Then he motioned for a pencil and paper, and I scratched in my purse till I found them. He carefully wrote down a new address, repeating each number and letter for the person on the other end. When he hung up, I said we should go back in the church and thank the priest. Sixto said he'd suffered enough already.

We followed the traffic noise and found another taxi. The driver took us to the address Sixto had written down. This time, there was no mistake.

There was a sprawling medical building with a small waiting room where a young woman in a white uniform sat behind a desk and pleaded for calm. The crowd spilled out of that room and onto the sidewalks. It looked like hundreds of people. They waited in small groups. Some waited in multi-generational tableaus, with grandmothers corralling the kids while Mom and Dad stood silently looking at the closed doors next to the office. Some were couples holding hands. Many were Latino, so you couldn't tell who was the US-citizen petitioner and who needed a medical clearance to get a visa. There were mixed couples, like us, including one family with a blond and rugged father who stood a head higher than his Mexican wife. Their three children stayed close. Anxiety was like a bad smell in the air.

But no gathering of people, no matter how glum they might be, fails to attract street vendors. Kids worked the crowd, selling *gorditas* from baskets. Old men on bicycle carts sold *paletas*. You could get a soda from a boy with an ice chest on wheels. Some people had white styrofoam cups of coffee, but I didn't see where they bought them. This was pre-Starbucks.

Inside the little room, the woman in white repeated her message over and over. *¡Por favor! Espera.* Just wait outside. She told us the same thing as we elbowed up to her desk. Sixto persevered. When she realized we'd just arrived, she waved toward the door and said our group was outside on the left. Our group? The people with appointments on Monday had to wait there, she said. They'd call us. Do you want our names? No. How can you call us without our names? Your group needs to wait on the sidewalk. She looked around us to the next person who was pressing her for answers she didn't have or wouldn't provide.

Sixto talked to a few people in the area identified as being from our group. He found out that the other group—the people crowding the office—had been there the day before. The X-ray machine had broken down, so they'd been sent away without the necessary documents. Their appointment letters ordered them to be at the embassy today. But, of course, they couldn't go without the X-rays. The medical technicians had the X-ray machine running again, and they were trying to process the people who had Friday appointments as fast as possible. The embassy, which was several miles away, sent word that the officials would extend the appointments a few hours because of the situation. They didn't say how many hours. The embassy gods were impatient, and there would be no appeal if they decided to slam the door before everyone was processed. Everybody knew this. If that happened, families would have to return to the United States without a mother or father. Everybody knew that, too.

I felt sorry for the Friday people. But I was more concerned about us. The stakes were too high to be gracious. If medical personnel in that building didn't get to us, I might go home without a husband.

Sixto was calm. It would all work out, he said. I tried to believe that. But all I saw was chaos. I had no idea how all these people were going to be processed before the day was over.

A young woman in a white uniform came out periodically to call in a group of ten Friday people to be X-rayed. They came back out one by one to wait with spouses and children. Every so often, another young woman in a white uniform would come out a different door with an armful of brown envelopes. People stopped talking when she started calling names. Men and women pressed forward, their families poised to run for the waiting taxis as soon as they had the envelope in hand.

Those whose names had not been called by the time the young woman ran out of envelopes would close in on her, calling out questions as she backed into the office and shut the door. Then there was more waiting. Sometimes the doors didn't open for a very long time.

It was midafternoon when someone came out and announced that they were going to start doing the blood tests for the people with Monday appointments. They wouldn't say if that amounted to a promise that they would stay on the job until our X-rays were taken, too. But lining up, giving names, and waiting for yet another door to open was a helpful distraction. At least we were making progress.

By late afternoon, the last of the Friday-appointment people were handed their envelopes and took off for the embassy. No one knew if the doors had been locked. But the Monday people were more interested in the doors to this building. We'd been good sports, but patience was wearing thin. There were whispered prayers and curses. We waited, as we had waited all day. After what seemed like a very long time, they began processing our group.

We won the lottery. We got the X-ray.

It was Friday night, so we decided to head down to the tourist district and get a nice dinner. The cabs were expensive, so we took a bus, which cost about twenty-five cents and came with entertainment. A young man with a guitar got on with us. He sang his way from the front to the back of the bus, weaving past the passengers who were standing in the aisle. Then he slung the guitar over his back and made the journey once again, this time holding out a plastic cup into which people dropped coins. He got off at the next stop. A few stops later, a clown got on and did some tricks.

I kept the envelope full of our papers for the embassy on the table next to me at dinner. Most of the time, I had my hand on it. Anyone watching would have thought that envelope was full of hundred-dollar bills. In truth, it was far more valuable.

By the time we finished eating, the tourist shops were closing, and the bars were getting rowdy. We decided to head back to the hotel. The last thing I wanted was to see my precious papers spilled all over the street because some party-hearty San Diego college student staggered into me on his way from one bar to the next. I felt a sense of relief as we rode the bus back to our weekend home. Friday had been a quest. But we survived and we had the prize. Now we just had to wait out the weekend.

Later, in our room, we began to realize that might not be so easy.

There was a lot of unusual activity in the room next door.

"Must be drug dealers," Sixto said. He didn't think much of my suggestion to call the hotel management. He made sure the door was locked and turned off most of the lights.

We could hear the people next door loading up vehicles in the little carport between our room and theirs. As soon as one drove off, we'd hear another vehicle pull in. Most of the time, they didn't even kill the engine. We'd hear shuffling and thumping and men calling out to each other. Then the slam of vehicle doors. We lay low on the bed, watching a snowy television and hoping the police didn't show up for a shootout. Eventually they got quiet and we fell asleep.

After a day wandering around town, Saturday night was the same. I fell asleep while Sixto watched the door and the guys in the next room loaded up vehicles.

We thought about returning to the Church of the Sneezing Priest on Sunday, but you never want to examine a miracle too closely. So we wandered around the tourist shops again, then sat in the plaza. Just like old times in Nogales.

The room next door was empty that night, but I didn't sleep much. I was up before dawn—and apparently before the water heater was turned on, too. I took a very cold shower before we got a taxi to the embassy.

When we arrived, it was another mob scene. People were lined up all around the building. Hundreds of them. Everyone's appointment letter must have said 8:00 a.m. When they opened the door, an officer looked at our letters one by one, verified the date, and sent us into a very large waiting room that had rows and rows of uncomfortable chairs. One entire wall was made up of windows like an old-time bank. Each window had a number. Behind each window was a federal officer who would review your papers, ask some questions, and give thumbs up or thumbs down. We watched people as they were called to different windows. Some agents spent more time. Some seemed to always send people away crying. Some looked friendly.

"I hope we get that one," I'd say.

"I hope we don't get that one," he'd say.

We were called to a window with a stern woman.

"Do you speak Spanish?" she asked me.

"Not really," I said.

"Do you speak English?" she asked Sixto.

"No," he said.

"Then how do you communicate?"

I thought we'd blown it right there. If they were looking for sham marriages, this was more suspicious than not knowing each other's favorite color. We'd just told her that we couldn't even talk to one another. She was thumbing through our stack of papers.

"We have a Spanish-English dictionary," I offered. "We use that."

"What language do you want to do the interview in?" she said.

"English," Sixto said.

She asked Sixto how he entered the country.

"There was this hole in the fence," he said.

She asked a few more questions—I don't even remember what they were. I do know that "gray and maroon" was not one of the answers. She looked us up and down. Then she said we could go back and sit down.

As we took our seats, I asked Sixto if we'd gotten the visa. He didn't know, either.

Before another family was called to her window, I hurried back to her. She had her head down, dealing with some paperwork.

"Excuse me," I said, "Did we get the visa?"

She looked up. I felt really stupid.

"Yes," she said. "Wait for them to call your name."

From then on, the waiting was easy. Whining kids and crying babies were no longer irritating. The snail's pace at which the hands of the big clock were moving didn't matter. We'd be going home together. We made small talk with people who were also giddy with relief. Dumb jokes. Mundane comments about how we should have eaten breakfast. Hopeful suggestions about where we'd have lunch. Time passed. Then we talked about where we'd have dinner.

It was well after dark before we arrived at the office where Sixto would pick up his permanent resident card. From there, we'd walk across the line together. Legally.

They called his name and gave him the treasure we'd been seeking. He had his green card. Then the federal officer took the pile of papers that I had been guarding all weekend and chucked the entire stack into a great big trash can. My jaw crashed. Collected over months and compiled according to an elaborate set of instructions, those papers had been our most important possession. Now they were garbage. Just like that.

We were among the last of our group to leave. The once-bustling room was nearly empty as we gathered our belongings. Then the back door, the one through which our group had entered, swung open and another big group of people entered. Tired kids dragged their feet. Babies whimpered. Weary parents shushed them as they found seats in yet another waiting room.

The federal agent who had tossed out our papers looked at his partner: "Where the hell are they all coming from?" he said.

Mexico, I thought, and you'd better get used to it.

This was the new Ellis Island. These new immigrants were walking away from one country and taking a chance on another one, just like my grandfather did when he left Germany. Just like my great-grandfather did when he left Ireland. Like Sixto, my great-grandfather came across the border illegally. But in his case, it was the Canadian border.

Years later, I would attend a conference at which a Mexican official told a room full of journalists that "America is pregnant by Mexico and doesn't know it." He objected bitterly when I put that in print, probably because it sounded undiplomatic. Many Americans see this as a threat to America. I'm not one of them.

CHAPTER SIX

Getting pregnant was, in fact, very much on my mind. The doctors had nothing but dire pronouncements when I finally decided to find out why it was taking so long.

Just as my fellow journalists had once relegated me to the "more likely to get killed by a terrorist than married" category, the elite class of medical professionals from whom I sought comfort now told me the old biological clock had wound down. I'd entered early menopause. No need to learn how to knit booties.

I was crushed. Defeated.

Sixto, however, dismissed the doctors' dire warnings. He told me to have faith. When I broke into tears at an outdoor event that was swarming with other people's toddlers, he said not to worry. He told me he had the mind of Jesus Christ, and that meant nothing was impossible.

My sister told me to get a bottle of Lydia Pinkham tonic.

"There's a baby in every bottle," she told me. It wasn't easy to find, but I got some.

My mother pointed out that there were probably lots of babies in Mexico who needed to be adopted.

My dental hygienist suggested a bottle of wine.

We worked day and night on the effort—but that part was for the sheer pleasure of it. The anxiety came each morning when I hoped to feel that telltale nausea—and didn't. My unhappiness rose each month as I saw my desire to be pregnant washed away on a tide of red. That's when I felt worst. I hid my sorrow from Sixto as much as possible. He was unconcerned and fully confident that God had set out the appropriate timetable.

Meanwhile, we began planning our first trip to Mexico. Now that he had his papers, Sixto could take me to meet his mother. This would have been somewhat stressful under any circumstances. But I got a very misleading idea of what it would be like from Sixto's sister Ana and her family. They stopped for a visit and turned my nervousness into panic.

Ana's husband Manuel is a minister in the Mennonite Church in Mexico. He was trained by the missionaries there. Because he showed promise, they arranged for him to study in the United States. The whole family had spent a year on a church scholarship at a seminary in Kansas. They were headed home now to Mexico, and Ana, Manuel, and their two children were going to stop in Tucson to visit us on their way back.

They didn't give us much advance warning, but Sixto and I spent the days we had planning menus and deciding where to take them. I thought the Desert Museum and Old Tucson were essential stops. We also arranged to get the single-bed mattress back and got extra sheets so the kids could sleep on the couch.

This was a big deal. This was the first time I would meet any of Sixto's family.

We wouldn't all fit in my Toyota Tercel, so I waited at home while Sixto went to pick them up at the airport. As it turned out, their luggage wouldn't fit in my car, either, so they had to store it at the airport. Arriving with only a few items in a plastic bag didn't deflate Ana's spirits. She and Sixto blew through the front door on a gale of laughter. They told and retold the story about arriving at the tiny car with suitcases too big to even fit past the opening of the trunk. Ana's laugh was a preview of her mother's. A pure unfiltered delight, like her life view.

She told me—Sixto translated most of it—that she'd gained a lot of weight in Kansas, but it didn't bother her. She was going to tell everybody that because she was so much bigger, her welcome home had to be bigger, too. She spoke in a singsong cadence that was pleasant to hear even when I couldn't understand what she was saying. The children were beautiful. I combed the little girl's long hair and braided it, wondering if I'd ever have the chance to do that for my own child. Self-pity was making a nest in my own hair—something Sixto warned me to guard against.

Manuel did his best to feather the nest, though it may not have been as malicious as it felt.

Like Sixto, he was a man of faith.

But Manuel's God frowned a lot and was a stickler for rules. Manuel's interpretation of those rules included modest dress for women—no pants, no jewelry—and obedience to the leadership of the male head of household. Seriously.

It was clear to me that Manuel's old-time Jehovah would deny my desire for a baby out of a stern, fatherly desire to teach me a good lesson. Or sheer meanness. Manuel would find that decision just. After all, I was thirty-five when I got married, and I'd worn a lot of earrings. Nor was that my only sin.

After Sixto told Manuel that we were attending the Disciples of Christ Church, rather than Tucson's Mennonite Church, his face went brittle. I was a bad influence, no question about it. Clearly, there would be celestially decreed consequences for my ill-considered choices.

The trip to Old Tucson was a mistake. I shelled out a lot of money to get us all tickets without realizing none of them had been raised on *Gunsmoke* or *Have Gun*, Will Travel. They found the western stuff boring. The sun was so hot that the kids wanted to leave in fifteen minutes. We huddled in a tiny patch of shade to eat the sandwiches I'd prepared for a picnic. They were not a hit, either. I'd forgotten that bread is no substitute for tortillas.

The next morning, I fixed breakfast. Another mistake.

I didn't know that serving watermelon and milk at the same meal was considered unhealthy. Sixto had one of his "Oh, that's right!" moments when Ana reminded him. Once the offending melon was removed, there was the challenge of the orange juice. I fought to keep my astonishment hidden as I refilled the sugar bowl so Ana could finish spooning three tablespoons of sugar into each glass of the fresh-squeezed juice that I'd paid a premium to buy for her family. The toast was also a flop. Sixto saved the meal by rushing to the kitchen to heat up tortillas and fry up some beans.

After we finished, Ana told me how wonderful everything was and thanked me profusely. Like Sixto, she doesn't do irony, so her praise was sincere. After all my work, she told Sixto, I should relax. She and her daughter would wash the breakfast dishes. My authority in the kitchen had been greatly diminished; my protests were useless. I bowed to her insistence that I have another cup of coffee and sit. Sit! Sixto and the little boy were in the back, practicing some soccer moves.

So I went to join Manuel in the living room.

He was standing. I stood, too.

Now came the hard part. What to say?

I had to be careful. I didn't want to give Manuel another reason to take word back to Mexico that Sixto's new wife was a jeans-wearing Jezebel who had led their beloved Sixto into a false church. The language barrier made it hard to go much beyond the small talk that we'd already exchanged at breakfast. I knew Manuel spoke some English; I just didn't know how much. He was cagey about that. He hadn't said a word in English, yet. He gave no hint of how much he understood of what Sixto and I said to each other in English.

So we stood there. When Manuel looked at my earrings, I could feel the metal getting hot.

I raised my cup to Manuel: "¿Más café?" I offered.

"No, gracias," he gave it the kind of formal emphasis you use in Spanish 101.

I could hear the kitchen noises and the sound of Ana's lyrical directions to her daughter. The backdoor was open, and there was the murmur of Sixto's rich voice as he explained something to the little boy. I would have gladly excused myself to join either of them. But I was rooted by a desire not to appear rude. If I'd gone outside, Sixto would have said, "Where's Manuel? Did you leave him alone?" If I'd gone into the kitchen, I'd have gotten a similar response. My duty, at the moment, was to entertain Manuel.

I wanted to succeed. But I didn't feel very entertaining.

We stood across the room from each other. The empty couch gave mute witness to our awkwardness. The morning light through the front window was behind him. I smiled. He cleared his throat. Then he spoke to me in English for the first time.

"Linda," he pronounced my name in Spanish, "LEEN-da." I

thought I detected a note of irony, but it could have been my imagination. "Tell me," he said, "do you have the Egyptian disease?"

This sounded like the prelude to a joke. But Manuel was not a jovial man. Or maybe I had misjudged him. It's so easy to ascribe motives to someone whose language you don't understand.

I kept my smile in place, but it did not feel any more natural. Was he trying to build a friendly relationship? Okay, I would laugh uproariously if he got to a punch line—no matter how bad the joke.

"The Egyptian disease?" I said. "What is that?"

He took his time. He let the sounds from the kitchen and the backyard drift back into the room. He waited so long I almost repeated the question. Then he spoke.

"You get it," he said slowly, looking directly into my eyes, "and nine months later you are a mummy."

I took the punch line right in the solar plexus. And I didn't laugh.

"No," I said.

But he already knew that.

I doubled up on the Lydia Pinkham that evening.

CHAPTER SEVEN

I was not pregnant a few months later, when my mother drove us to the airport to catch our flight to Los Mochis. Sixto still wasn't concerned. He assured me that God—the smiling, happy God who brought us together—would send us a baby soon enough. Nor was he concerned about what his mother would think of me.

I, on the other hand, was concerned about everything.

I had fretted about my clothes. I didn't want to reinforce the image of me that Manuel had surely presented to Sixto's mother. Maybe I shouldn't take my Levi's, I said to Sixto. Why not? he responded. Maybe I shouldn't wear my jewelry. Why not? They'll love you just as you are, he told me. He wasn't being much help.

So I compromised. I took my jewelry—bracelets and earrings—but I went shopping for what I considered to be more suitable clothes. My suitcase was full of long skirts, dowdy blouses, and sensible shoes. My travel outfit was a too-long circle skirt and jersey blouse. I'd forgotten all about the beautiful, shining women I'd seen emerging from those humble houses on our trip to Copper Canyon. I was ready to walk into a nineteenth-century frontier outpost. A fundamentalist one, at that.

I certainly looked odd as we walked through the little Los Mochis airport. The Mexican women my age wore high heels and stylish dresses—the kind of clothes I would have worn to work. Even the old ladies were more elegant than my new, simplified version of me. Sixto didn't seem to notice or care that I had transformed myself, although he probably would have rather presented me to his family as the modern, professional woman he'd married.

He treated me with the same courtly manners, the same deference. He insisted on carrying all the suitcases, a bag on each shoulder and one in each hand. He still managed to open all doors and wait as I walked through.

We took a taxi to downtown Los Mochis. From there, we would ride a bus to his mother's house. He gave careful instructions—even though we'd ridden the bus in Tijuana. When the bus arrived, I was to get on first and take a seat in the front. He'd follow with the luggage and pay for both of us. If there were no seats in front, he said, I should just stand there and wait for somebody to get up. Under no circumstances was I to go more than a few rows back. It didn't matter how many empty seats were in the back, I was not to sit there.

I laughed. Why not?

Just don't go back there.

Why?

He seemed uncomfortable about this, but finally he told me, with lowered voice, although no one near seemed fluent in English. He said the back of the bus was not a place for nice women. It's where the drunk men sat. They had no respect and no shame. He was careful to explain that he knew I was not the kind of woman who would ever willingly sit near such a man. He just wanted to make sure I didn't go back there by accident. He didn't want people to think I was the kind of woman who didn't care if men looked at her in a disrespectful way.

Unlike Manuel's opinion of my clothes and jewelry, the opinions of strangers on the bus mattered a great deal.

I waited on the busy sidewalk with the suitcases while Sixto spoke to some of the drivers in a long line of buses at the side of road. Most of them had hand-lettered signs in the windshield that the suggested destinations, but Sixto didn't have much confidence in how often those signs were changed. When he got confirmation from the driver of the Los Suárez-bound bus, he came to carry the bags.

I climbed aboard ahead of him. It was standing room only at the front, so I waited while he juggled the suitcases and paid the driver. Before he was done, a young man touched my elbow as he stood up to surrender his seat. There was another man in the window seat, but he looked sober and this was the second row, so I figured it would be okay. I thanked the gentleman and sat down.

Then I found out there are few strangers in this part of Mexico. The young man who'd stood up helped Sixto hike our suitcases onto a shelf over the seats. After a few pleasantries, they started excitedly calling each other *hermano* and clapping each other on the shoulders. After they shook hands, Sixto begged my forgiveness for his bad manners and introduced me.

The young man extended his hand with great courtesy and spoke his name. It is the custom to tell someone your name as you shake hands, but it is a custom I didn't yet fully understand. I wasn't expecting a name. Even if I had been expecting it, I wouldn't have recognized the way he said it.

"Xavier," he said. Ha-VEE-air.

I thought he was trying to speak English, but mixing up his syntax with some iffy pronunciation. I understood him to say: "How you are?" I thought it was cute that he was trying to speak to me in my language. I also thought I was terribly clever of me to have figured out what he said.

"Fine," I replied in English, as I shook his hand. "How are you?"

He must have thought it a rather odd name. But he smiled and went back to his conversation with Sixto. He and the man sitting next to me got off at the next stop, so I scooted over so Sixto could sit down. He told me the young gentleman had been a member of a church youth group he'd help organize years ago.

"What's his name?" I asked. Sixto gave me a perplexed look.

"Xavier," he said.

Oh. Ha-VEE-air.

I grew up not far from the Mission San Xavier del Bac. I'd been saying that name for years. But I sure didn't recognize the way this fellow said it. I felt a flush of linguistic dread. Sixto and I always spoke English.

The practice of saying your name when being introduced gave me trouble even after I figured out where I went wrong with Xavier. My name is an adjective in Spanish. People use it to describe things of beauty; they don't use it as a name for their children. Saying "Linda" when shaking hands could be taken as a commentary on the person I was meeting or an egotistical declaration. Either way, it felt awkward.

In truth, everything felt awkward, even though Sixto was doing his best to be an attentive host.

Sixto was right about the condition of the men at the back of the bus. Despite a number of empty seats, no woman ventured back there. Even the other men preferred to remain in front, standing if necessary.

We met two other people who recognized Sixto on that trip, which took about forty minutes once we got out of town. One man was a distant cousin; they didn't call each other hermano. The other man did call him hermano, but he was not a relative. He was from the church.

We rode past vast agricultural fields and little clusters of houses made of mud or adobe blocks. Along one stretch of divided road, there were several men cutting tall grass from the median. They tied the bundles onto the handlebars of their bikes. This was to feed the pigs, Sixto told me. There was excitement in his voice. He was looking at a familiar landscape, getting ready to share his world. This was his home.

These were houses like the ones I'd seen from the train and wondered about. To me, the scene was still quaint, like a travelogue. To Sixto, this was the normal that he had carried with him as he tried to make sense of modern America.

We crossed a bridge over the Rio Fuerte and saw cranes standing knee deep in an eddy made bright green by floating plants and algae. Sixto said the river used to be much bigger when he was a child. He told me they would swim there and collect firewood along the beaches. Now there were dams upstream; the Rio Fuerte was a tame river.

The bus bounced over a speed bump, crossed another bridge that spanned a wide irrigation canal, and turned left.

"There's Toñita's house," my husband said.

I knew this sister from phone calls and stories.

"That's Tía Chayo's house," he said. I caught a glimpse of a cluster of houses behind a massive cottonwood tree that had exposed roots as tall as the bus. She wasn't really his aunt. She and his mother were cousins who had been raised together after his mother's parents died.

We were passing through a village.

"Is this where your mother lives?"

"No," he said, "This is Cohuibampo."

The bus lumbered over another speed bump at the edge of town, then picked up speed. Next stop was Los Suárez. I felt as though my stomach was in a vice.

What if they hated me?

Sixto's English sounded strained, like it wasn't what he wanted to be speaking in this place. Sixto had immersed himself in my world. He had rejected opportunities to attend a church with services held in Spanish and he only rarely tuned in to the Spanish TV channels. He'd worked hard at ESL classes and became so fluent that he would begin taking college-level classes in English that fall. But here, I'd be the only one who understood him when he spoke English.

I scanned my brain for phrases that might be suitable to greet Sixto's mother. She was waiting to meet her tenth child's American wife. I didn't even know what I would call her.

CHAPTER EIGHT

The bus bucked as the driver downshifted. I staggered toward the front door as Sixto followed, juggling the bags and urging me to be careful. We stopped. The door opened and I picked my way down the steps. Sixto followed, taking a long time to properly thank the driver, who had pulled up right in front of Doña Sole's house to let us off.

There was a shallow, weedy ditch between the road and a three-strand barbed-wire fence. Through an opening in that fence I could see a dirt yard and rosebushes covered in enormous flowers of all colors: red, pink, orange, and yellow. Towering over them were trees with leathery leaves and green fruit that looked like elongated baseballs. They were mango trees, but I didn't know then then. Nor did I recognize the giant avocado tree that was part of the canopy high overhead. How different from those little houseplants my mother and I had coaxed from seeds held by toothpicks over jars of water.

The blue sky through the leaves, the sun: these things were the same. But everything under those trees was new to me as we walked up a pathway toward the house.

Doña Sole's new house was only partially finished then; construction would resume when money was available to buy materials and labor. The walls were adobe block between supports of concrete beams. The roof was a slab of concrete. There were open rectangles where the door and windows would one day be installed.

"¡Mamá!" Sixto called out.

Two women rushed through the doorway and another jumped through an opening for a window. The one who came through the window was yelling "¡Sixtito!" But she was too young to be his mother.

They were all rushing toward us. But which one was my mother-in-law? Sixto dropped the bags and rushed into the embrace of all three. The ladies wept and exclaimed and hugged Sixto, dried their eyes on their sleeves or dish towels, and hugged Sixto again. They looked at me. I had no idea what to do.

Sixto looked toward the house and called out again "¡Mamá!"

There she was.

Doña Sole was a head shorter than my husband, solid, but not fat, with long grey hair pulled into a ponytail at the base of her neck. Her cotton dress had a pattern of tiny pink flowers. My grandmother would have called it a housedress. But instead of the heavy lace-up shoes my grandmother would have worn with thick stockings, Doña Sole wore plastic flip-flops. She stood in the doorway, wiping her hands on a frayed kitchen towel that hung over her shoulder.

He ran to her and she fell into Sixto's arms and began weeping. This was exponentially more intense than the greetings from the other women. This time, the world stopped. As they embraced, she wept and exclaimed things like "¡Gracias a Dios!" and "¡Mijo!" Sixto wept, too, and said things back to the top of her head, which was buried in his chest.

After what seemed like a very long time, the earth began to revolve around the sun again. Kids ran from behind the house. More voices could be heard exclaiming my husband's name. A big truck chugged down the highway, followed by another bus, its gears protesting the sudden downshift at the speed bump.

Sixto reached out to me over his mother's shoulder, still weeping. The other ladies shepherded me forward. When I got close enough, he pulled me into their embrace. It was a tight hug, and all I could do was hold on.

I tried to return the intensity of their moment. But I was unaccustomed to such raw emotion. It washed over me, but did not sweep me away. My eyes stayed dry, and I felt a twinge of guilt about that.

In a few moments, the hug loosened and I stepped back. Doña Sole looked at me and said something I didn't understand. I smiled.

Then she pulled me into a hug that included just the two of us. There was more weeping, more exclamations. When I got the chance, I smiled again and nodded at her. She seemed entirely satisfied, and we began another round of hugging.

I had not said one word, but I'd been accepted.

From that moment on, whatever I did—whatever harebrained, outlandish, North American request I might have—was just fine with Sixto's mother. I was part of her family and under her protection, as surely as a chick under the wing of its mother hen.

It took a long time to sort out everybody else. As Sixto introduced me, I did my best to grab names and hold on. But he would get pulled away by this person and that person, and I got lost in the labyrinth of relationships. Siblings. Spouses of siblings. Children of siblings. Neighbors.

One of the older ladies who'd been first out the door was Doña Mariyita. She lived next door and shared coffee with my mother-in-law every afternoon under the mango trees.

The woman who jumped through the window shouting "¡Sixtito!" was Emilia, Doña Sole's youngest daughter. Emilia and her toddler daughter were living with Doña Sole, but Emilia spent much of her time out with a woman friend, leaving the baby, Anayetzi, to Doña Sole's care.

Toñita, whose house we had passed in Cohuibampo on the way in, had exited the house in a typically more dignified manner after their mother and Sixto were embracing. It was clear even then that Toñita would inherit the mantle of family matriarch, even though she was not the oldest daughter. She had gravitas. Doña Sole cited her opinions often and with finality. If Toñita said it, you'd better listen.

Several of Toñita's five children flocked around the house with the other nieces and nephews.

Sixto's older brother Trini and his wife Nelly were also there to greet us. They had a young son and twin baby boys.

There were other people—matriarchs and children. I was still trying to keep them straight when Doña Sole ushered us into the house for something to eat. They'd been cooking all day.

Sixto wanted to give me the grand tour first, and show me where we could wash the travelers' dirt off our hands.

Doña Sole's house was a complex of structures. The doorless entry of the new house led to a living room that was dominated by a large dining table with chrome legs sticking out from under a flowered plastic tablecloth. A bare light bulb hung from wires tacked to the ceiling. That room opened into the kitchen, which had an old wooden worktable, a set of unpainted wooden shelves, and a tiny white enamel stove. A pipe ran through a hole in the wall and linked the stove to a big butane tank outside. Two small bedrooms opened off the side of the living room, with curtains hanging in the doorways. In the daytime, those curtains were scrunched together and hooked over nails so the air could circulate. At night—or if somebody was changing—they were pulled closed to provide privacy. Doña Sole slept in one room, which had another small room attached. This is where she planned to put a bathroom—just as soon as running water and a sewer were available. Emilia and her daughter slept in the other bedroom.

Sixto's youngest brother, Luis, also lived at home, but he wasn't there that day. He had a job at the Hotel Santa Anita in Los Mochis, the graceful hotel where the gringo travelers took refuge after the Great Bus Robbery. It was a good job, but even a good job in Mexico didn't pay much. Doña Sole said Luis was restless and thinking about checking out life on *el otro lado*.

Luis slept in the old house, which was just a few feet outside the back door of the new house. This is where Sixto grew up, and he was excited about showing it to me.

The walls were made of cactus ribs and mud; the roof was corrugated metal tacked down with nails hammered through bottle caps. Sixto said the bottle caps helped prevent leaks. He was proud of this old structure, where he and eleven of his siblings had been born and all fourteen children had been raised.

Sixto's father had built the old house, but everyone helped maintain it.

As a child, Sixto would help Toñita rub the walls and dirt floors with water, turning the clay-laden dirt into slurry that dried hard and smooth. It created a surface firm enough to sweep—lightly.

If you applied too much pressure, the shell would break and the dirt became powdery. This is something I learned from experience; the new house had dirt floors for years.

I could smell the damp earth as I stood at the doorway of the old house. The light from the door illuminated a homemade folding cot on the opposite wall. It had wooden legs and a brown burlap sling. Grey blankets were folded on top, and our suitcases had been lined up carefully next to the blankets. I hadn't noticed when someone picked them up from where Sixto dropped them in the front yard during our dramatic entrance. The corners of the room—there was only one room—were dark, but I could see the edge of another cot. The floor around it was strewn with men's clothes. My husband grumbled at the mess Luis had left.

Behind the old house was the outhouse. This was an intimidating little shack with tippy sides and a black tarpaper roof. When Sixto unwrapped a rusty wire from around a nail, the door dropped open with unbalanced enthusiasm. He said there was another nail inside so you could wire the door shut for privacy. The floorboards had gaps. Sixto tapped his foot on a few of the boards to determine which were solid enough to be safe. He told me I should check my footing before closing the door and shutting out the light. The big spiders in the corners looked slow and uninterested in visitors.

"I'm sorry, *mi amor*," he said, as he wired the door shut. "I'll look for a better one."

"It's okay," I said.

We headed back toward the new house. On one side of the kitchen door was an ancient wooden table covered in dirty dishes. This was the sink. While we were inspecting the outhouse, Doña Sole had poured some hot water from her teakettle into a bowl and set it there. Sixto retrieved a bar of soap from the shower, which was on the other side of the kitchen door, and we washed our hands.

That shower was a cubby built of strips of wood and plastic sheets. It abutted the adobe wall of the new house. Inside the shower, two five-gallon plastic pails were sitting on wooden planks. A pink-and-white plastic bowl floated in one of the pails, which still had water in it. Getting clean was about dipping and pouring. The outside of the white pails was dirty—mud splashed from the floor. But they were clean inside. Sixto replaced the bar of soap next to a bottle of shampoo that was balanced on a flat rock.

Also behind the house was a woodstove cut from a fifty-gallon barrel. There, my mother-in-law had a huge pot of beans bubbling. She fed long chunks of mesquite wood into the fire incrementally, all day long. It gave the place a wonderful smell, and took the dampness off early morning trips outside. Sometimes she heated water there to wash clothes in a concrete tub that stood next to the shower and drained into a ditch along the side of the house.

It would be a lie to say I didn't long for the Hotel Santa Anita, with its brilliant white sheets and spotless bathrooms. But those conveniences were much farther than just a forty-minute bus ride. Going to the hotel would have brought embarrassment to Doña Sole and shame to Sixto for acting like he was too good for his family. I longed for the hotel the way a waitress longs for a winning Powerball ticket. A nice dream, but not likely.

The accommodations at Doña Sole's were supplemented by warmth, laughter, and mountains of good food. As we ate our first meal there, I reminded Sixto that he'd promised to call my mother when we arrived. I thought he'd been a bit hasty in making the offer; now I was sure he'd made a mistake by leaving her with the expectation of a call. There was no phone.

As usual, he didn't look the least bit concerned. He and his mother exchanged a few words and he held out his hand for me to follow.

We went through the back yard, over some weathered boards that were bridging a narrow irrigation ditch, through a field dotted with cows and cow pies, under a barbed-wire fence, over another makeshift bridge, across another narrow irrigation ditch, and into the yard of Trini and Nelly's house. Sixto stopped to check out their outhouse, and informed me it "wasn't bad," if I needed to use it. So I did.

When I emerged, Sixto was chatting with Trini and Nelly. But since we'd just seen them at Doña Sole's house there was no need for elaborate greetings. After a quick hello, we were on our way.

We crossed their yard and turned onto a dirt road. We walked into an enormous, collective embrace. People emerged from open doors calling Sixto's name. They clapped him on the shoulders and shook his hand, calling him hermano and saying *Dios le bendiga*. No one was surprised when he introduced me. Everybody already knew. But they were sure interested in having a look at this exotic US-born wife.

I was warmly greeted with touches on the shoulders and handshakes. After each encounter, we would walk a little further and Sixto would fill me in: that one was his sister's husband's cousin, this one was an assistant pastor at the church, the other one had helped him lead the church youth group, another was the son of one of the men who used to go to the ocean with Sixto's father once a year. They would come back after several days with shark meat in sacks of coarse salt.

My husband was a rock star in this community, and his fans obviously had missed him.

Until we took that walk, I never thought much about what Sixto left behind when he crossed the border to marry me. I always assumed that what he found on my side of the line was infinitely superior to whatever he'd left behind. Who could not prefer a reliable toilet to a rickety outhouse?

Now I saw something more impressive than good plumbing. Here was an outpouring of genuine friendship and respect that left me breathless and humbled. The lives of the people of this ejido were woven together in elaborate patterns. There had been a Sixto-sized hole in that tapestry. Their welcome back was unbounded. What's more, they had plenty of goodwill left over for me.

As Sixto's wife, I got instant respect in his community. What a contrast that was.

As my husband, he'd been viewed with curiosity, reserve, and maybe even a little suspicion by my friends. At the newspaper, people took odds on how long the marriage would last. In the community? Aside from my landlady, the neighbors around our duplex never even noticed a change.

Sixto must have missed this feeling of being connected to all these people. But he never mentioned it during those months of learning English and taking long walks down streets where the only greetings came from pleasant strangers. He had more relatives than I could keep track of. But during those dinners when he and my mother and I sat around her small table on her desert acre, he acted like the three of us constituted a complete, and very special, universe.

A little further on we arrived at a little wooden kiosk that was unpainted and had no sign. On the counter was a glass jar full of brightly wrapped candy. On the back wall were shelves sparsely populated with grocery items. It reminded me of the place where Dottie found the Miracle of the Eyebrow Pencil.

The woman tending this store knew Sixto. Of course. They conversed enthusiastically for a while. I smiled and nodded. My smile muscles were tired, though. My brain was so overloaded I'd almost given up trying to figure out what people were saying. My pride hurt from being so rumpled from the trip as I met people to whom my husband was a hero.

Besides, weren't we supposed to be calling my mother?

After a few more pleasantries, the woman reached under the counter and pulled out a black rotary phone and placed it in front of me. Sixto told me what numbers to dial to get out of the country, and I made the call. The sound of my mother's voice and the brief conversation in English was as refreshing as a cup of hot tea. It was a reminder of a world of reliable plumbing and other wonderful things. I missed my creature comforts even in the arms of a warm and welcoming society.

When I hung up, Sixto gave the woman in the kiosk some money for the phone call, and we started back to his mother's house. Over the years, the location of the sharable phone in the community changed. But there was always somebody who had a landline and was willing to share with those who would reimburse the cost of the call.

Cell phones have changed everything now; everybody has one. Now there are official stores with metal signs that advertise beer. But that day, this woman in the wooden kiosk was the local communications specialist. She was the evidence of how much I had underestimated the options available to the people of Los Suárez. When we got back to Doña Sole's, she made me a cup of tea.

Later that evening, we followed nearly the same route to church, which was painted a cheerful blue. Inside, the rows of wooden benches filled up fast. I recognized some people from earlier that day and offered the appropriate salutation. I was always on the lookout for family members because they required special attention, better hugs, more attempts at conversation. For neighbors, a handshake and a smile might suffice.

I was sure most of the ejido had been at Doña Sole's that afternoon. But I was wrong. There were many new people here.

As we took our seats, I was looking forward to some quiet time when everyone would be focused on the service instead of Sixto and me.

Trini began by leading everyone in a song. Sixto excused himself and joined his brother at the front. Then the preacher launched into a long discourse. It didn't take long to realize he was talking about us. He called on God to bless our visit. He rejoiced that we'd arrived safely. He said something I didn't catch, and everyone turned to look at me. Sixto bounded over, beaming with pride, and led me to the front of the church. We stood there while the preacher prayed over us and members of the congregation called out "¡Si, Señor!" and other affirmations.

The preacher took a seat. I sensed that I was supposed to do something, but I had no idea what. I looked at Sixto for guidance. He was flush with the moment and just grinned back at me with a kind of goofy proud-enough-to-explode look. We stood at the front of the church and Sixto talked about how happy he was to be back and to introduce everyone to his "*esposa Linda, muy linda.*" This really made me feel the weight of the long trip and lack of opportunity for a shower. He held my one hand in front of him and clapped his other hand over it from time to time to punctuate what he was saying. I tried to smile at the right times, and look humble when the mood switched to praising the Lord and being grateful for so many things.

Eventually, Sixto led me back to my seat and then rejoined Trini to lead the congregation in more songs. I did my best to hum along, thankful that I was no longer the focal point.

A boy about ten years old squeezed in beside me. He'd been at Doña Sole's house that afternoon, lurking around the edge of the activity and watching me intently. He had rushed to help when my purse spilled onto the table. One of the things he'd picked up and handed back to me was a retractable ballpoint pen. Yellow plastic. Cheap. He looked at it with such longing as he held it out that I told him to keep it.

"*Un regalo*," I said. A present.

This was my Lady Bountiful moment. I not only remembered the right word, I also indulged in a First World fantasy about the power of my gilded lifestyle to transform the needy. Maybe that pen was all this child needed to become the next Carlos Fuentes. I would get credit in some ledger in heaven—maybe I'd hear him recall my kindness on some talk show after he won the Nobel Prize for literature. Yes, he'd say, it all started that day when a kind North American woman gave me her pen. . . .

He had the pen in his hand when he shoved in next to me at the church. The congregation was still singing, but this kid tried to engage me in conversation. I shushed him gently, but he went right on talking. A woman in front of us turned around and said something sharp. He shut up then. But he didn't stop trying to get my attention. He started drawing on his arm with the pen I'd given him. I tried to ignore him, but he would tap me every once in a while and nod at the ink scribbling on his arms. I sighed. He just needs a little guidance, I thought.

He stopped and watched as I felt around in my treasure-chest purse for a piece of paper. I handed it to him, miming that he should use the pen on the paper, not his body. He let the paper fall to the floor and looked at me with a cocked-head grin. Then he went back to drawing on his body. No longer Lady Bountiful, I was now a corrupting influence. For about the nine-hundredth time that day, I had no idea what to do.

This was really uncomfortable.

When Sixto came back to join me, the boy darted off to sit against the wall. He remained in my line of sight, drawing on his arm again whenever he saw me looking.

Sixto later told me the kid was called Güero, which means light or blond. He was neither when I met him, but once upon a time he might have had the kind of soft brown curls that surrounded Emilia's daughter's face. Nicknames hang on in Mexico. That's why some people called *Gordo*, which means fat, aren't really fat, and so many people still call my husband Sixtito, which means "little Sixto" even though he is all grown up and his namesake father is long since dead.

Güero was the grandchild of Don Nito and Doña Mercedes, who lived on the west side of Doña Sole in a tiny mud house. Unlike the other houses, this one was always closed up tight. There was no door, but a ragged gray blanket hung across the opening like a keep-away sign. If there were any windows, they were sealed blind. I rarely saw Doña Mercedes, but Don Nito spent his days sitting on a low chair near the wire fence that separated his property from Doña Sole's. My mother-in-law warned me to stay away from that side of the house. When I asked why, Sixto explained that when Don Nito needed to urinate, he didn't bother to get up. He just aimed at the bushes along Doña Sole's house and let rip.

For our arrival, Don Nito had brought over two very large grapefruits from a tree in his yard. His wife followed him at a respectful—or perhaps safe—distance. Don Nito completely ignored me and everybody else when he presented the grapefruit to Sixto. His wife clasped Sixto's elbow, and my husband greeted her with great interest and respect. She said little and looked very nervous.

Doña Sole went through the house to the pan over the fire and dipped some beans into a bowl. She handed it to Doña Mercedes after Don Nito started walking home. She made sure her husband wasn't looking, then Doña Mercedes tucked the bowl behind her scarf and followed him back across the fence. Güero stayed behind.

He was their daughter's child.

Sixto told me that he remembered the daughter from school, but he hadn't seen her for years. No one had. When she was growing up, people said she wasn't "right." She was always a little confused and hesitant. Don Nito was a harsh man and he treated her with particular contempt. Like the rest of Don Nito's children, she left as soon as she was old enough. Unlike Don Nito's other children, who never came back, the girl's escape was unsuccessful. She returned beaten up and pregnant. Don Nito let her stay, but he never let her forget. She remained in the shut-up house even in the hottest days of August, when the temperature hit 115 degrees and the humidity was almost that high.

As Güero grew up, he would sneak over to Doña Sole's for food and human kindness. He told Doña Sole that Don Nito often ordered him to hit his mother. The boy told Doña Sole he didn't like to do it, but he was scared not to. After I heard that story, I really didn't want to eat Don Nito's grapefruit. But Doña Sole said his tree gave the sweetest fruit in the ejido, and she was right. They were delicious.

Güero came around a lot the first few days we were there. He was fascinated with me, but he tried to get attention by doing things like throwing food on the floor and pulling things out of my purse and running around the house with them. Doña Sole would ignore his weird behavior and offer him food; she'd been doing that for years. But he didn't listen to her anymore. One of his more unpleasant behaviors was to sit quietly in a corner until I forgot he was there, then he would run at me and put his face about two inches in front of mine and tip his head from side to side. He also liked to mimic my Spanish, saying things like "*¿Como se dice?*" over and over while staring at me. Sixto tried talking to him, but eventually he gave up and told the boy to go home and not come back.

A couple of years later, we found out that he ran away from Don Nito's house of horrors and started living on the streets in a larger town. It wasn't far away. Don Nito knew where he was, and he knew the boy was begging food to eat. But the old man never went to get him. Eventually, according to the gossip, Güero fell in with drug dealers and began doing their dirty work—he'd been primed to embrace cruelty.

My pen offered no redemption. Neither did Doña Sole's compassion. Don Nito died about six or seven years after I first met him. Doña Mercedes sold the property and moved away with the daughter. Nobody heard from them again. There was some discussion about whether we should buy the place and add it to Doña Sole's property. I didn't want that place at any price.

It reminded me of Boo Radley's house in *To Kill a Mockingbird*, but without any redemptive spirit. Just unrelenting sadness.

The people who did buy the property tore down the shack where Don Nito terrorized his family. They built a two-story house that blocked Doña Sole's view and raised suspicions because it was so opulent. That kind of money didn't come from just washing dishes on the American side of the line, people whispered.

On our first night at Doña Sole's, Sixto and I dragged two cots out of the old house where Luis slept and set them up in the living room of the new house. It was Easter time, so it wasn't cold—even without door or windows. It was too early in the year for mosquitos, so that wasn't a problem, either. The bedding that looked so dingy when I saw it sitting on the cot in the old house didn't look any better up close. But it was clean and soft, and it smelled fresh.

After our cots were made up, we went outside to brush our teeth in the front yard. It wasn't much past 10:00 p.m., but the village was asleep. The night was quiet except for an occasional tractor trailer that downshifted loudly before lumbering over the speed humps at the edge of town, only to pick up speed again in front of Doña Sole's house. The stars were almost as astonishing as the ones in Cerocahui.

We went inside and Doña Sole retired to her room after turning out all the lights. It was the first night since we'd been married that we hadn't slept in the same bed. But the cots were too small for two, and we weren't planning on having sex with Sixto's mother on the other side of a cloth curtain. We held hands across the wooden frames of our cots and went to sleep.

CHAPTER NINE

Early the next morning, I was awakened by a thumping under my cot. Sixto poked around in the corner and something rather large and dark emerged and hopped under the table, which had been pushed up against the wall to make room for our cots. Doña Sole, who was in the kitchen making tortillas, stuck her head around the corner to see what was going on. She came over and gave Sixto a hug and kiss. Then she did the same for me.

"*¿Como amaneciste?*" she said to me.

Oh, God, I thought. What does that mean? I could have dealt with ¿buenos dias? or ¿dormiste bien? But I had no idea what this meant.

Sixto was poking around under the table.

"¿Como amaneciste?" she said, again. A little louder, just in case volume would help my understanding.

I looked to Sixto. He wasn't paying attention.

My first morning and I was distinguishing myself as a complete idiot.

"Mamá," he said, then added something that got her attention.

She looked under that table and threw her head back, laughing and slapping her hands on her thighs. She looked at Sixto and laughed again. Then she went outside. When she came back, she was holding a shovel that appeared to have had its digging surface worn in half. Instead of a nice long blade with a straight edge, it was stumpy and had two short bulges with cleavage. She carried it purposefully in front of her with both hands.

"Don't kill it," Sixto said in Spanish.

She thrust the shovel under the table. When she pulled it back out, there was an enormous toad sitting on it. She held it out for inspection. It sat there blinking its eyes in the light, not moving. It continued to sit calmly as my mother-in-law walked out the back door. We watched her through the hole for the window as she crossed the yard, holding the shovel in front of her. The toad sat looking ahead, as though it were taking a ride through the countryside in a fine carriage. All it needed was a crown and a princess. Instead, the creature was unceremoniously dumped under a key lime tree at the corner of the yard. Doña Sole rushed back to turn her tortillas.

In less than a minute, she brought me one, fresh from the *comal*, and went back to get another for Sixto. We sat on our cots and tossed the tortillas to cool them. Yes, they were amazing.

The breakfast that followed consisted of more food than I normally eat in an entire day. Beans, eggs, sausage, more tortillas, and instant coffee, which always seemed entirely unworthy to accompany the laboriously prepared food Sixto's mother served us. I grew up thinking instant coffee was for rushed mornings when you didn't have time for something better. My mother would never have served it to guests. But Doña Sole presented the cup brimming with hot water, spoon laid across the top, and jar of instant Nescafé as though it were a really big treat.

After breakfast, Sixto suggested I might want to take a shower. His brother would arrive soon to take us to the beach. I put everything I thought I'd need in a plastic shopping bag and took a towel to the cubicle behind the house. I was supposed to undress in the little stall with the curtain firmly shut, and then put the same clothes back on. You never knew if Don Nito was sitting in his chair just the other side of the fence. A robe was out of the question. One needed street clothes to walk out the back door—even if one were only going into the shower. When I was finished, I went into Doña Sole's room to change into clean clothes.

Things got more complicated when I tried to dry my hair.

The plug on my hair dryer had one large prong and one narrow one. It didn't fit into the socket in Doña Sole's wall. She got a pair of heavy-duty wire cutters from on top of the chifforobe in her room, and prepared to do surgery on the prongs. Sixto intervened. He gently told her that if she trimmed the plug, my hair dryer wouldn't work when we got home. She shrugged, put the wire cutters away and came back with an extension cord that had the appropriate slots. Its prongs had already been modified to fit into the wall socket. It worked with her radio, her iron, and her blender, she said. It also worked with my hair dryer.

I couldn't see much in the tiny mirror on the wardrobe, and the room was always at half-dusk—the curtains on the Don Nito side of the house permanently pulled tightly shut. Every so often, Sixto would pop in to see if I needed anything. When I told him I didn't have a bathing suit, he laughed. He said I wouldn't need it.

"Are we going skinny-dipping?" I said.

"Skinny, what, mi amor?" he said.

Then someone called to him from the other side of the cloth curtain and he left me alone in Doña Sole's room. I wanted to look my best, but that was out of the question. I took a deep breath and pushed my way through the curtain into a bustle of greetings.

Toñita and her family had arrived with Sixto's brother Rosario, known as Chayo, and his family. These two families lived in side-by-side houses in Cohuibampo.

Chayo had Sixto translate as he told me that the name of their town means "Pig in Mud." He thought that was very funny, and he wanted me to share the joke.

Chayo, six years older than Sixto, was the family clown. He kept everyone around him laughing. His wife, Luz Maria, was the sister of Toñita's husband Gavino. Luz Maria was regal, with high cheekbones, a strong character. But her sense of fun was equal to her husband's. She and Chayo kidded and teased each other like newlyweds, despite being the parents of a boy of about ten and two littler girls. Sixto told me Chayo made good money selling seed for agriculture. The tangible proof of his prosperity was in the elegant clothes his family wore and the truck in which he would drive us all to the beach.

I greeted everybody, including what seemed like a classroom of children who now called me Tía.

As Doña Sole continued to cook breakfasts for the new arrivals who were hungry, Toñita, Luz Maria, and Nelly were putting supplies in bags and cardboard boxes at her direction. The kids carried things out to the men to load on the truck.

When we finally pulled out, Chayo was at the wheel, with Luz Maria, Doña Sole, and Toñita sitting next to him. They tried to get me to squeeze in up front, too. But I decided to ride in back with Sixto, Trini, Gavino, Nelly, and the kids.

Sixto and I stood, waving over the cab of the truck as we backed out. Doña Mariyita and Emilia waved back from the front yard. Emilia looked forlorn. Her little girl, still wearing footed jammies as the day grew warm, sat in the dirt. We had plenty of room in back for them, but as Doña Sole reminded Emilia much earlier that morning, the baby wasn't ready to go.

The beach was about an hour's drive and a universe away from my experience.

It was as pretty as any travel brochure: light sand and an ocean as blue as the sky it reflected. But this was not one of those Mexican beaches you see in tour magazines. There were no Americans sipping margaritas here. No *palapa* umbrellas. No vendors hawking crazy hats, keychains, and sunglasses. No college girls in itsy-bitsy bikinis. No bronzed young men flexing their muscles.

This Mexican beach was for Mexicans—and I'd never seen anything like it.

Rows of trucks were lined up facing the water. Most were surrounded by chairs and tables under do-it-yourself shade structures. Chayo maneuvered the truck into a line and we all climbed out. The kids headed for the water, and were called back to help with the work. First, we had to put up a ramada off the side of the truck. I recognized the sheets and blankets they pulled out of the bags we'd been sitting on. They had been on Doña Sole's bed that morning. The wooden poles they shoved in the sand were the ones Doña Sole used to prop up the wire clothesline that stretched across her yard. There was efficiency and familiarity in the technique they employed to put up the shade structure. They'd done this before.

Next, we unloaded a table and piled it high with bags of food, jugs of water, bowls, knives, and cutting boards. Chayo went right to work cleaning shrimp, dumping them into a big bowl.

Everybody was cutting vegetables or chopping cilantro for the ceviche. My job was slicing key limes in half and squeezing them over the growing mound of cleaned shrimp and vegetables. Toñita stirred. Doña Sole poured in a handful of salt. Chips were brought out. Sixto tried the ceviche. More salt, he said. It was poured on and mixed in. He tasted again. He said nothing, but got more chips and tasted again. And again. And again. Doña Sole laughed and put away the salt. Then they shooed Sixto away and covered the bowl of ceviche with a wet towel.

It was time to go swimming. Only Gavino stayed behind to keep an eye on things.

We moved en masse, weaving around the rows of trucks parked in front of us until we reached the hard, wet sand at water's edge. The kids exploded like hot popcorn as the first wave hit their feet, then charged into the water, shoes, clothes, and all.

Doña Sole didn't wait for a wave to christen her feet, she went right in, moving with steady strides as the water rose to her knees, hips and waist before she plunged in and swam—fully clothed in her calico housedress and plastic shower shoes. All around us, people were going in and out of the water, laughing, splashing, swimming. There wasn't a bathing suit in sight. So this is how the Mexicans do it, I thought.

When Sixto and I reached water's edge, we stood there hand in hand. He looked at me and then at the water, with an impish smile. We began slowly walking in. The water pulled at my long skirt. By the time we were chest deep and bobbing in the waves, I remembered that I had two $100 bills sewn into the lining of my bra. My emergency stash. My North American angst manifest in folding money. I told him about the cash. He laughed and held up a hand, his not-waterproof watch dripping.

Our companions were unencumbered by burdens like excess cash and watches.

Doña Sole was swimming with the waves. Toñita was calling to Rosario and Luz Maria, who were tossing one of Doña Sole's flip-flops back and forth. The kids were swimming after the other one as it disappeared and reappeared in the waves. Sixto's mother didn't seem to care if she ever got her shoes back.

The moment was timeless and full of infinite possibilities. Under that glorious spring sun, soggy cash and ruined watches were of little consequence.

On this Mexican beach done Mexican-style, nobody worried about immersing their street clothes in salt water. Nobody had to worry about how they looked in a bathing suit, either. This was liberating.

People who arrived in crowded trucks prepared their feasts on the spot and devoured their food—like we would—while shivering and dripping seawater. Nobody had remembered towels. But that realization would come later.

Right now, in the water, in the sun, there was only this moment—and it would remain warm and joyful years later, even in the dark of winter, even when getting along was hard work instead of child's play.

We sparkled in the water. Sea jewels.

On the way home, Chayo pulled off the road at the edge of a field to buy a crate of freshly picked strawberries from a roadside vendor. We went directly to his house, where, Sixto told me in English, they had a flush toilet and an indoor shower. I was giddy at the news. I spent a glorious five minutes enjoying that shower until the biggest cockroach I'd ever seen came walking across the wall.

The rooms of Chayo and Luz Maria's house had stuccoed walls painted cheerful colors, and they had furniture fancy enough to be quietly condemned by Toñita as *vanidades*. Luz Maria was criticized for making Chayo work too hard so she could buy things like a carved wooden dining table and matching chairs, and a living room suite that had an overstuffed couch, a loveseat, and a glass-topped cocktail table.

Luz Maria also had a washing machine on the front porch. But Chayo didn't pay for that. She'd bought it, Sixto explained, with money she made by selling cookies. Sixto called her a "virtuous woman," only half in jest. He admired her spunk and her initiative.

By the time I got out of the shower, Luz Maria had a strawberry cake in the oven and she was passing out a blended drink (non-alcoholic) made with strawberries, milk, and ice. This was a dilemma for me.

I always went by my mother's rule for safe travel in Mexico: never eat fruit that couldn't be peeled. This strawberry drink could make me very sick unless Luz Maria had washed the berries in purified water. But after enjoying Luz Maria's bathroom, how could I quiz her about how she'd washed those strawberries? Maybe Sixto could figure a polite way out.

I thanked Luz Maria for the drink, and I caught his eye. He was standing across the room holding his own glass of strawberry beverage. He glanced at the half-full box of strawberries on the counter and gave me a look of deepest regret. I sighed. At least he understood. That made all the difference. I decided I would do this for him. I began to drink, comforted by the knowledge that my sacrifice would not go unnoticed. My husband was so keenly attuned to my thoughts and needs that he understood the situation without a word from me. Wow, I thought, what a guy.

The truth, revealed later while reminiscing about the day, was far less romantic. Sixto hates strawberries, something I hadn't memorized before our trip to Tijuana. He wasn't expressing sorrow for my dilemma—he was looking for sympathy from me. That drink put him in the same position I was in: consume or appear ungracious. Neither one of us wanted to consume.

I drank mine—and didn't get sick. Sixto hid his behind some dirty dishes and didn't worry about it. He did the same with the strawberry cake when it got passed around. What a guy.

Before we left, Luz Maria said she wanted to give me some roses. This was a little surprising, because Doña Sole had a front yard full of blooming bushes. But I followed my sister-in-law through the house and into a garden where I could see rows of rosebushes waiting like heavy-uddered cows for somebody to relieve their burden.

Luz Maria began cutting the best flower of each color and handing it to me as I exclaimed over their beauty. They really were magnificent. Toñita came out and clucked about how I was going to hurt myself with the thorns. She took the roses from me and hurried into her house, returning with the stems wrapped in wet paper.

Luz Maria asked Toñita's permission to get a sample of a particular red rose from her yard, and we crossed an invisible barrier. Their yards were side by side. I couldn't tell where one rose garden ended and the other began. The houses were very different, though.

Unlike Luz Maria's big, bright house, Toñita's house was a tiny mud structure. The open door revealed a small table—no shelves, no counters—and a treadle sewing machine draped with cloth. The rest was hidden in darkness.

The five of us squeezed into the wide front seat of his big truck as Chayo drove us back to Doña Sole's. When we arrived, Emilia's daughter, Anayetzi, sat crying in the dirt of the front yard. She was still in her pajamas. Doña Sole carried her into the house, and we heard Emilia yelling. Sixto went in, and the arguing stopped.

Then he came out to help unload the truck, shaking his head when I asked what was wrong. We were saying goodbyes to Luz Maria and Chayo when Emilia came rushing out. She stopped to greet us all with hugs and kisses, breathlessly explaining she was off to meet a friend. She rushed off toward the bus stop on the other side of the road, the one that leads to Los Mochis.

Inside, I found Doña Sole holding Anayetzi and stirring some beans on the stove. She'd taken off the unseasonably hot pajamas the child had been wearing all day, leaving the toddler in just her cotton panties. The little girl's hair was damp with sweat and her face was red from crying. But she looked content now, her arms around her grandmother's neck, watching the beans bubble in the frying pan. Sixto spoke to Anayetzi and she held out her arms to him. We took her into Emilia's room and I helped him look around for clean clothes. She was a beautiful child with a great smile. After we got her dressed, I took a picture of Sixto feeding her.

"Two and a half and she's still being fed?" my mother observed, when she saw the picture.

Emilia came back later that evening with a woman friend. Both tried to embrace Doña Sole, but my mother-in-law did not return the other woman's greeting. Doña Sole made no secret of her dislike of this woman, remaining unusually quiet and completely ignoring Emilia when she said they were hungry.

The roses were lying on the table, their stems still wrapped in the wet paper. Emilia's friend picked them up.

"*Son de ella*," my Doña Sole said coldly. The words translate as "they are hers," meaning me. The tone said: "Leave them alone."

The woman continued to finger the roses. She said I needed to press them, and asked Emilia for scissors. Emilia asked her mother to bring them, and Doña Sole grudgingly complied. The woman cut the blooms off the stems and stuck them between the pages of a magazine I'd brought from the United States. By the time she was finished, the magazine was bulging with ruined flowers.

The atmosphere in the house was poisonous and unusually quiet. No joking, no laughter, no cooking noises. Sixto had been as silent as his mother. This limited the conversation to one woman who didn't speak Spanish very well and two who didn't speak English. Emilia and her friend quickly gave up trying to ask me things. Without Sixto to translate, it was a slog. Even when they spoke to each other, their voices sounded hollow in the larger, disapproving silence of the room.

After Emilia left to walk her friend home, Sixto spoke to Doña Sole in urgent but respectful tones. I could tell he was quizzing her about Emilia. How could you let her run around with that woman? Their mother was uncomfortable, but tried to shrug it off. She said "mijo, mijo" a lot and looked very tired.

Emilia's behavior was not something she could control. But she would be held responsible for it; her neighbors would think less of the family because of it. This was Sixto's biggest worry. The family's good name was a valuable commodity that belonged to all of them. Emilia had no right to do anything to devalue it. Doña Sole already knew all these things. She was weary that evening, and not just from the sun and ocean. Sixto told her to go to bed. He said he'd wait up for Emilia and lock up after she got home.

When Emilia arrived, she sweet-talked her way past the lecture her big brother had planned and went right to bed.

CHAPTER TEN

The next morning, Doña Sole threw the magazine and the murdered roses in her trash pit to be burned. I gathered up the rose stems from under the table, where the woman had kicked them, and got a nasty scratch from the thorns. Toñita had been wise to wrap them up.

Sixto was in the kitchen, heating up water for my shower. He said I might want to get dressed early because the family was on the way. Yesterday had been a prelude. This was the day everybody was coming to see Sixto and meet his new wife.

They came by foot, bus, truck, and car. The women showed up in freshly pressed outfits of spring pastels with nice shoes. Jewelry might be forbidden, but fancy buttons and lace collars were not. They were elegant, with styled hair and perfect makeup.

I, on the other hand, was a mess. The humidity left my hair fully bedraggled, and I had nothing nice to match the dressy outfits Doña Sole and the other women were wearing. Nevertheless, when I was ready, Sixto demonstrated beyond a doubt that love is blind. He put his arm around me and he introduced me to everyone with heaps of pride and unbounded enthusiasm.

We pulled chairs and cots out of the house as more and more people arrived, and placed them in an ever-widening circle under the mango trees. Sixto made sure I always had a seat next to a beloved sister, aunt, or cousin. Not that I spent much time sitting. Doña Sole would announce each new arrival as soon as she saw who was getting off the bus.

"¡Aquí esta Isabel!" she'd proclaim, and we'd rush over to say hello.

Those I knew—Toñita, Ana, Nelly, Luz Maria—had arrived very early to begin doing things in the kitchen.

Their children were nicely dressed and under strict orders to stay clean. The boys had parts in their hair as sharp as the creases in their pants. The girls had tight ponytails tied up with ribbons and bows. They walked carefully to keep the powdery dirt from turning their black patent-leather shoes beige. The older children carried around the babies and kept the toddlers amused with quiet games on the cots.

Sixto's brother Porfirio pulled up too fast in his truck and jumped out with the panache of Vicente Fernández getting off a horse. He wore high-heeled cowboy boots, Levi's that rode just below his growing belly, a cowboy shirt with snaps, and a Stetson. He yelled his greeting across the yard to Sixto.

Riding with him were his four beautiful daughters and one son. The boy, the youngest, was called Jesus because he was the one Porfirio had been waiting for. It was hard to decide which of Jesus's older sisters was prettier. They were charming, gracious, and called me Tía as they complimented my hair and my blouse.

Charming girls, I thought.

Their mother, Artemia, had arrived by bus much earlier to help with the cooking. She was not a Mennonite like most of the family. She was a Seventh-day Adventist, and all the children were active in that church. She was in the kitchen, and she stayed there.

Porfirio had a statement to make about his machismo and he gave everyone a chance to hear it. The idea that somebody might not appreciate him never crossed his mind.

He gave his mother the obligatory *abrazo* and turned his attention to Sixto and me. I got a hug and a look that was vaguely reminiscent of that bus driver with the shrine on his dashboard to the Virgin of Guadalupe and the non-virgin of his dreams. Porfirio's once-over was not impolite, though, and I did not take offense. I was his brother's wife, and while he might offer opinions about my appearance when I wasn't around (something he did with other brothers' wives), I got his full respect. That did not, however, preclude curiosity about the things that mattered.

He came right to the point: Was I pregnant?

When Sixto said no, Porfirio leaned close to him: you have to turn off the TV, little brother.

I laughed almost too loudly. The lack of a baby had nothing to do with lack of trying, but I didn't say that. Nevertheless, Porfirio joined me in laughing. There was nothing sanctimonious or solicitous about him. Nothing complicated. His personality was big enough to have its own gravitational pull. I couldn't help liking him.

Porfirio had a plastic bucket of fish and a device to cook them that looked like a wok on legs. He built a fire in the middle of the yard and fried those fish—heads, tails and all—as Trini and Sixto chopped tomatoes, onions, and cilantro, and mixed up salsa at a table under a tree. The rest of the meal—tortillas, shredded lettuce, beans, and macaroni salad—was being prepared in the kitchen.

Porfirio sent one of the kids inside to get a plate with tortillas, then gave me the first fish. He showed how to peel off a chunk of flesh carefully to leave the bones behind. He laid the fish in the tortilla and added salsa fresca, lettuce, and beans. Fish tacos. Porfirio asked me how it was.

"*¡Maravilloso!*" I said, using a Spanish word that should have been easy to understand.

Porfirio asked Sixto to translate.

The idea that I might be able to speak Spanish did not compute for Porfirio. So Sixto told him I said it was marvelous, and Porfirio hooted his approval.

There were dozens of people there that day. At one point I got my camera and gathered everybody together for a picture. I piled some rocks on a table, balanced the camera on top, and set the self-timer. I was taller than most of the women, lighter, and less elegantly dressed. But we were all smiling in the dappled shade of Doña Sole's trees. And we were all well past full of good food.

For the rest of the week, we settled into a routine that began each day when Doña Sole brought us warm tortillas while we were still cozy in our cots. Then came the enormous breakfast and instant coffee.

Routine chores took up the rest of the morning. The bedding had to be folded and put away because the cots were either used for other things during the day or folded and leaned against the wall. Those huge kettles that were used to cook beans and the cast-iron pans where the eggs were fried and the beans were refried had to be washed in bowls of heated water behind the house. It was a challenge I took on without fully believing it was possible.

Then there was shopping. A few kiosks around the village sold eggs, lard, and other necessities. But they were very pricey. A bus ride into the slightly larger town of Ahome for a few groceries was a morning's excursion. Traveling into Mochis to go to the supermarket took pretty much all day, and included being jostled on crowded streets with armloads of plastic shopping bags.

It also included visits.

While we were there, we went to see the wife of Sixto's elder brother, Jilberto. Sixto gave credit to Clara for raising children who were scrupulously respectful. Sixto had stayed with this family years ago when the children were younger, helping Clara with the chores. Her fondness for him was obvious.

Even though we arrived unannounced, she immediately began making tortillas and sent one of the children to the store to buy the ingredients for a big meal of fish, beans, and salad. Her generosity probably cost a week's worth of groceries. But we were family, and hospitality was a matter of honor.

When Sixto asked about Jilberto, Clara said, "¡Ah, Sixtito!" Then the conversation moved on.

On the way back, we got off the bus at Cohuibampo to visit Tía Chayo, who was Doña Sole's cousin. Like Porfirio, she had her own gravitational pull. It just pulled in a different direction.

Her house was the first built and the smallest of a cluster of homes behind that enormous cottonwood tree that we saw on the ride in that first day. Tía Chayo's married daughters had built homes around the original house. The size and quality of the building materials reflected the types of jobs the husbands held. Some were mud. Some were brick.

Entertaining was done in Tía Chayo's home because she was the matriarch.

Her living room was bigger than Doña Sole's, and it had a suite of real living room furniture perched over the dirt floor. On the wall was a large oil painting of Tía Chayo that had been done by an itinerant painter when her face was unlined and her dark hair had no gray. She looked severe in the portrait, stern and unbending. In real life, she was either laughing, mopping tears with a kitchen towel, or gripping my hand while looking deeply into my eyes to ask God to bless me and my family. The artist had not captured any of her energy.

Tía Chayo's oldest daughter, Magda, wore the lace cap of the Mennonites. She lived in the big house. Chuyita was most like her mother: her big eyes danced with mischief and she loved to talk. The youngest girl, Petra, was petite and quiet. She and Sixto seemed to have a special bond of friendship. The daughters all brought in their children to meet me and shake hands with all of us in turn. They were shy and painfully polite.

As we left, Tía Chayo hugged Doña Sole and me with feeling. But when she got to Sixto, she had to stop and sob into her towel.

"¡Sixtito, Sixtito!" she cried, clutching Sixto's hand and calling down all sorts of blessings and prayers.

He'd been on a long journey to a faraway and dangerous place, she told God. Now he was going back there. She would have preferred it if we built a house on Doña Sole's property so Sixto could once again bring his testimony to their churches and communities—and her family. So we could raise our children with her children's children. So Sixto and his wife could be part of their lives, their church. There would always be a place for us there, she said, among people who loved us.

She was talking to God. But she wanted me to listen in, too. She was hoping I would decide to share Sixto with them. To bring him home.

Doña Sole must have had these thoughts, too. But she never laid it out so blatantly. In fact, I got the idea that she was glad Sixto's opportunities had expanded. Maybe it was just my imagination. Both Tía Chayo and Doña Sole treated me with great affection. But I think Tía Chayo saw me as someone who had taken something wonderful away from her life; Doña Sole saw me as someone who had brought wonderful things into her son's life.

Tía Chayo walked with us to the cottonwood tree with the gnarled, exposed roots. They had been impressive when passing on the bus. But standing next to that tree was a study in feeling small. Far, far above us, the leaves rustled.

I took a couple of pictures and the others—except for Sixto—looked a bit surprised. Did I want the kids to stand by the tree? A picture of somebody made sense. But a picture of that old tree?

We made our final goodbyes and walked up the road a short distance to Toñita's house. It would be unthinkable to be this close and not stop in.

We sat outside under mango trees for yet another cup of instant coffee. A pig was tethered under a cottonwood tree downwind from the house, and one of the children carried a bowl of table scraps and dried-up tortillas to the animal. Toñita said if we came back at Christmas time, she'd turn the pig into barbacoa for a celebration.

From across a hedge of roses and poinsettias, Luz Maria waved as she loaded clothes into the washing machine on her porch. She was proud to be seen doing the laundry; other women used concrete scrubbing tubs like the one outside Doña Sole's kitchen door.

After awhile, Luz Maria came over to sit with us for a few minutes.

It was nearly dark when we caught the bus back to Doña Sole's.

After a day like that, I would have called out for pizza. But Doña Sole changed into her housedress and began making tortillas. Sixto helped. I drank a cup of tea.

I had made a polite pretense at being interested in learning how to make tortillas. My attempts at rolling out the balls of dough brought gasping cackles of laughter from Doña Sole: they were *zapatos*, shaped like shoes, or *calsones*, shaped like underwear. She was not mean-spirited about it. She knew as well as I did that Sixto could make perfectly good tortillas. He told her that it was enough for one of us to have the skill. She agreed, and whether she meant it or not, she sounded convincing.

The day-to-day demands of her life were well beyond my abilities. She knew that. And I suspect she also knew that I had skills at other things. At least she acted that way. She never made me feel uncomfortable about not being a skilled tortilla maker. She never tried to lure me into trying again.

It was a lot harder to get out of making tamales.

Aside from mixing the masa—a duty delegated to the most highly skilled person in the room—tamale making was simple assembly-line work. Everybody had to chip in. This is what we did our last day in Los Suárez.

The entire day.

It started before the roosters announced morning. I woke up on my cot to see Doña Sole sitting at the table in the predawn dark. She drank a single cup of sweetened instant coffee. When she saw me watching, she patted my head and told me to go back to sleep. Then she stepped outside and began pulling ears of corn from a plastic sack. One by one, she ripped off the husks and cut the kernels from the cobs. The piles of husks grew bigger as the sun began to come up. She took the huge bowl of glistening corn and poured it into a cast-iron grinder mounted on an old tree stump.

Sixto and I were getting dressed, still blinking away the night, when Artemia walked over from the bus stop. We all said our greetings, but quickly. There was no time spent on breakfast, either. Artemia rolled back the tablecloth and began kneading lard on the brown Formica surface. She spread it thinly across the table, leaning into the palms of her hands. Then she cupped her hands and scraped it all back into a neat pile before repeating the process over and over. The lard became shimmery and slipped through her fingers like quicksilver. Liquidy: that's what Sixto calls it. When the consistency of the lard was just right, Artemia used her hands to mix in the ground corn and other ingredients. She'd ask Doña Sole what it needed and they'd squeeze and poke the masa before comparing their diagnoses and making a judgment about what to add.

Chile pods had been boiling on the stove. Sixto dumped the cooked pods into the blender with a little water and some garlic and onion. While I was looking around for the lid of the blender, he took the wooden board on which he'd cut the onions and held it tightly over the top of the blender.

"You can't do that!" I said as he hit the "on" switch.

The lidless blender whirled the mixture into a deep viscous red under the cutting board. I made a mental note to bring his mother a blender on our next visit.

Doña Sole called me into her room. There on top of the wardrobe was a pile of cardboard boxes she'd collected from the grocery store. She'd saved them to pack tamales for her daughters and daughters-in-law to take home at the end of the day. Some had originally held votive candles. Others had carried baby formula. They were good, she pointed out. Sturdy. I agreed.

Then she had me pull down two plastic boxes that had snap-on lids. These were store bought and never used. They still had labels. She said these were for us. She'd use one to pack tamales for Sixto and me. The other was for my mother. She patted the bed and I set them down there. We wouldn't need them for hours and hours, but she wanted me to know she'd been planning this for some time.

I followed her through the curtain and back into the living room, where Sixto and Artemia had determined the masa was ready. They covered it with a damp towel.

Next came the chicken, which had to be pulled off the bones and shredded. It had boiled the night before and been left on the stove to cool. Doña Sole didn't have a refrigerator then. Sixto said the chile would kill any germs. When his mom handed me a small bowl of the shredded chicken after it had been seasoned with the chile, the taste was enough to dispel any health concerns. If this killed me, it would be worth it.

The house filled up with sisters and sisters-in-law. Men came and went, some cousins, some neighbors dropping by to visit with Sixto. They sat on our sleeping cots or on chairs that had been pulled away from the table, where space was needed for the tamale assembly-line workers to stand. Women sliced carrots and potatoes into long strips. They trimmed the ends off string beans. Once cut, the vegetables were dumped into bowls of water.

Ana and Manuel arrived and all activity stopped as Doña Sole greeted them.

Manuel took a seat while Ana got him a cup of coffee. Sixto and I had a running joke about how Ana fussed over Manuel's coffee—doing everything short of drinking it for him—so we exchanged a knowing glance as the operation began.

First, Ana moved a kitchen chair next to where Manuel was sitting. Then she put a cup of hot water on the chair and spooned in the instant coffee crystals. She stirred. Then she got the sugar bowl, spooned some in and did more stirring. She added milk and stirred. Then she dipped up a sample and brought it to her lips, keeping her other hand cupped below the spoon to catch any drips. She tasted. Then she added more sugar and stirred again. She tasted. Then she put the spoon down next to the cup and told Manuel it was ready. He took a sip.

"How's the coffee," Sixto asked him, and I had to turn away to keep from laughing out loud. Manuel said the coffee was fine. Sixto then made a great show of asking me if I'd like a cup of tea. He went to the kitchen to put the kettle on, then brought me the cup with unnecessary fanfare. If Manuel knew that Sixto was delivering a lesson, he gave no indication. If anything, my brother-in-law looked slightly validated by this unseemly role reversal: clearly he'd been right to think something was amiss in Sixto's marriage.

Nobody else seemed to be paying attention, except Doña Sole. She waved me toward the chair next to Manuel, the one that Ana had used as a table for his coffee. My mother-in-law picked up Manuel's now-empty coffee cup, pulled the chair forward a few inches, and patted it. I sat and drank my tea quickly. By the time I was finished, the tamale production line was ready.

The table glistened where the lard had been kneaded to smoothness, but it looked dull and scratched when the rest of the cloth was removed. On one end, there was the big bowl of masa with the damp towel now folded back. Dried corn husks floated in bowls of water next to it. Then the chicken mixture. Then bowls of vegetables. The process was efficient. Somebody smeared a corn husk with masa, and passed it down to the next person, who would add a spoon of chicken and pass it on. Each tamale then got a strip of potato, a few beans, a slice of carrot, and an olive. At the end, it would be topped with another masa-lined husk and tied shut with strips of corn husk. The chicken mixture was juicy and Nelly would squeeze each tamale until the red liquid ran out before tying. The juice puddled on the table and dripped off, darkening the dirt floor.

The midmorning sun had turned the dawn mist into a sticky film that coated everything. Flies came in the open doors and had to be shooed from the food preparation area. They converged unmolested on the dark spots on the floor and erupted into nasty buzzing battles when someone walked past.

Sixto was bantering with Manuel and helping tie up tamales. He'd told Artemia to fix some without olives for me, and he was tying them a special way so we'd know which ones they were. Now he turned his job over to Emilia, while he got a clean towel to wave over the table to keep the flies away. He continued joking with Manuel, who remained seated.

My job was to add the green beans. I was new at this, so I asked how many beans. Toñita said one. A few tamales later, she decided one wasn't enough. I should put two. So I started adding two beans. A little while later, she said I was putting in too many beans. We might run out, she said. I went back to adding one long green bean to each tamale. Then Emilia said we had plenty of green beans. I should use more. Sixto asked Toñita how one could be too few if two were too many. Everybody laughed. From then on, I varied the number of beans I put in each tamale.

We made ten dozen tamales. They were stacked into a pan so big I thought the tiny gas stove would collapse under the weight. But it was used to this kind of load.

I thought we were done cooking. But then I noticed Doña Sole was fishing the remaining strips of potatoes out of the bowl, and Toñita was peeling and slicing up more. Ten dozen tamales were not going to be enough?

They fried up piles of french fries and Doña Sole served them with salchichas (wieners) that she was proud to say had been bought at the store fully made—not prepared at home. She handed the first plate to me. Soon we were all standing around the remains of the tamale assembly line, eating Doña Sole's version of American food. The pan with the tamales rocked gently on the stove, burping steam from under the lid every once in a while.

The table was cleared and the bowls and dishes were stacked on the old wooden table outside the back door. Leftover french fries and sausage ends were scraped into a dirty plate under that table. Doña Sole signaled to a thin dog that was lurking around the side of the old house. It paused. Doña Sole said something and it ran over, gulped down the food. It was not Doña Sole's dog, just one of many strays. But she fed this one, and chased away the bigger dogs.

"*Pobrecita*," Doña Sole said, as the dog loped off, her milk-filled teats wagging from side to side.

The cooking marathon continued.

This time it was Luz Maria kneading lard against the table. She was going to make *coricos*, Sixto announced excitedly. He loved those rich cookies as much as he hated strawberries. He told me about them in the first weeks of our marriage. His description of these little ring-shaped cookies made my mouth water. I was excited about the idea of giving him something that would remind him of home, and insisted he call Mexico to get the recipe. He said it was a good idea without telling me that one, there was no phone at his mother's house to call, and two, nobody in his family used a recipe.

When he didn't follow through, I continued to bring it up. Eventually, he called a family that had a telephone. It was not the same kiosk where we had recently called my mother, but it was the same system. They sent someone running for his mother and probably set off a community-wide alert that Doña Sole was about to receive momentous—likely terrible—news from her son in the United States. But as people gathered 'round to listen to her end of the conversation, they heard Doña Sole guestimate how much of each ingredient was necessary to make the cookies. On our end, I insisted he write things down. So it was only natural that Luz Maria, whose specialty was cookies, would make some coricos for us to take back to Tucson.

When she had the dough ready, the tamale-making team reassembled to roll and shape the cookies. In the United States, you sometimes find these coricos as almost doughnut-sized cookies. The ones we made were more like giant Cheerios—about the size of quarters. They are delicious little globs of fat that seek out your waist like guided missiles and linger there for decades.

Once cooked and cooled, dozens of cookies were neatly packed in a box lined with a blue and yellow kitchen towel. Doña Sole asked Luz Maria where she was going to pack the ones for *La Se-*

ñora, my mother. Luz Maria said they were all together; we could separate them when we got home. Doña Sole was not entirely pleased with that answer. She told me to be sure my mother got plenty of the cookies.

Toñita brought out a box of empanadas she had made the night before. These are flaky fold-over cookies with a filling made of sweetened condensed milk that is scalded into dark richness. I don't know if it is the lard or the love that goes into them, but those cookies could put the Girl Scouts out of business. Jenny Craig should give them away anonymously on street corners.

There was plenty of room in our suitcases for all this stuff because we'd brought down bags of candy and presents for each sibling's family. Tablecloths, bath towels, or sheets. I thought these were rather boring gifts when Sixto suggested them, but he said those items were pricey in Mexico, and the quality was much lower.

For Sixto's mother, I brought sheets and towels and a curtain that had the Last Supper depicted in lace. She immediately had Sixto put it up in front of the opening for the big window in the living room. Despite the lack of glass, it gave the room a more finished look and helped control the flies. Everyone who came in commented on it, and she proudly told them all that her *hijos*— her children—brought it for her.

She shut the sheets and towels away in the wardrobe. She did the same thing with the dishes and silverware we brought on subsequent visits, but in a different cabinet. She'd leave things out long enough to show visitors, then she'd lock them away. Sixto might insist she get out the cups to serve coffee to her guests, and sometimes she'd go along—reluctantly. But the next time we arrived, the cups would be locked away again behind the glass doors of the cabinet in the corner of the living room. Over the years, the cabinet became crammed full of things we'd brought. She continued to use the chipped and mismatched dishes and the bent silverware that had inspired me to bring her some nice new replacements.

In this, she was much like my mother. They each had a stash of gifts they considered too good to use. The difference was the threshold for specialness, which was defined by the economics of their households. There were a great many other similarities between my mother and Sixto's mother.

Doña Sole was a matriarch who had earned her position of respect in the community through years of honorable behavior. She knew the importance of following social rules and stayed within boundaries that some of her grandchildren would never learn or ever value. She violated social norms to do compassionate things like show kindness to someone the community rejected or defend stray dogs from mistreatment.

My mother also lived according to the rules of her time and custom. She also condemned cruelty that others ignored, and was perfectly willing to call "bull crap" when she saw it—regardless of the perpetrator's rank.

Both of these women valued family above all else. The big difference was in their communities and in the payback they got—or didn't get—from their respective cultures.

Doña Sole was living where she had grown up. The accumulated value of her virtuous life was like a bank account that had tangible benefits for herself and her children. She was a respected elder in a culture that valued old people. When my mother moved from her birthplace in Ohio to Tucson, she found a land of newcomers where there was little interest in one's personal history and contributions.

Age does not command the same respect in American culture as it does in Mexico, so as she got older, my mother's value to the society seemed to diminish. What's more, my mother's virtuous life didn't have much currency in her community because Tucson has a transitory population—at least in the series of apartments where we could afford to live until she bought that trailer. Her sense of herself as an honorable woman got her through many life crises, but there was no collective memory of it. No community record of her good reputation. No collective social payoff.

When Doña Sole prepared to send us home, neighbors gathered to join her and share the moment. When my mother left her home to pick us up from the airport on the other end of our journey, a neighbor might wave without much thought about where my mother was going or why. They weren't bad neighbors; they just had a different understanding of what it meant to live in a community.

Both my mother and Doña Sole had good lives. Neither would

have traded places with the other. Their similarities transcended their economic status and their nationalities; their differences were largely superficial or based solely on culture and experience.

I knew that my mother would appreciate the tamales and the plastic container as much as Doña Sole enjoyed sending the gift.

Our flight was early the next morning, so we would stay with Porfirio and his family in Los Mochis that night. We were packing up our suitcases as Porfirio arrived with his usual manly bluster.

His impatience to get us loaded into the truck didn't make the goodbyes any shorter or less tearful. He stormed around and acted like all this foolishness was keeping him from something important. But Doña Sole took her time, and so did everybody else.

Porfirio drove like a New York cabbie, only faster. This was breathtaking on the highway to Los Mochis, and downright awe-inspiring as he negotiated city traffic, engaging in numerous games of chicken with other drivers who thought they were man enough to back him down.

Porfirio always won.

He took us down a dizzying series of turns as the streets got narrower until the pavement disappeared into dirt roads. Porfirio and Artemia didn't live in one of the very poor areas where homes were tacked together out of cardboard boxes and other trash. But their neighborhood was well below the standard of those paved and scrubbed Mexican streets where North Americans look at the washed tile driveways winding through lush landscaping and think, "I could live here."

Most tourists from the United States would be afraid to visit Porfirio's neighborhood, and Sixto said that was just as well, because the taxis wouldn't come to this part of town if you called. Unlike the ejidos, where houses were surrounded by open space, the houses here were so close together that people could jump from one roof to the next, which thieves sometimes did to raid goods that were stored up there.

Many of the houses had pickets of rebar jutting up from the concrete roof in anticipation of a second story that would be added as soon as finances allowed.

Porfirio was among the generation that left rural Mexico, got decent jobs, and sent their children to city schools with the hope the kids would be able to climb permanently out of poverty. Unlike his mother's house, Porfirio's had tile floors and painted walls. There were wooden doors on the bedrooms. His indoor bathroom had a sink, toilet, and shower. There was running water in the kitchen, too. In the living room, two overstuffed couches faced each other across a chrome-legged cocktail table on which Artemia had placed a large arrangement of artificial flowers. It blocked conversation, so Artemia would move the flower arrangement when people sat on the couches. Behind the second couch was a big dining table, Formica-topped like Doña Sole's.

This is where the action took place.

When we arrived, Porfirio's daughters were buzzing around that table. As I mentioned before, it was hard to decide which was prettier. Maria de los Angeles was the oldest, about sixteen when I first met her. Her features made me think of Jackie Kennedy. Maria loved to laugh, often at her own expense. With Maria, you felt like you were sharing a private joke—maybe a little mischievous, but never naughty. Next in age was Viridiana, called Vidi. She had thick, thick hair, as black as a starless night. Her charm came from a remarkably gracious manner, but the cheekbones and the dark eyes didn't hurt, either. She was warm, enthusiastic, and projected a sincere interest in those around her. Her happiness was contagious. Jacqueline was next. She had fair skin and light brown hair that fell smooth and soft around her face. She was also the most serious, showing great—and genuine—concern for whether her tíos needed a glass of water or something to eat. Her cheekbones were sprinkled with freckles, and her eyes were hazel. The youngest was Yahira, who had the bone structure of an Aztec princess and bobbed hair that suited her impish attitude.

When we arrived, the girls were getting ready for an event at the Seventh-day Adventist church. Like the Mennonite churches in the ejidos, the city churches had extensive programs for the youth, and Porfirio's daughters were active participants.

They all stopped what appeared to be frantic preparations and waited while each greeted us in turn. These were no quickie greetings that said, "You've interrupted something important." They were elaborate and thoughtful salutations that included inquiries about our well-being and hunger level. They only went back to their mad dash to get ready when Artemia reminded them the clock was ticking.

And then it was a mad dash.

Maria hurried off to shower as Vidi went back to ironing her dress on a towel that had been laid on top of the dining room table. Yahira angled for an opportunity to use the iron to touch up the collar on her dress. Jaqui rushed to the back bedroom, her head wrapped in a towel, emerged with her hair cascading luxuriously, searched for something, then dashed back to the bedroom. The next time we saw her, she had her hair in an elegant knot at the back of her head. Maria came out of the shower and Yahira ran in. Eye makeup. High heels. One more chance at the iron. Their T-shirts and shorts gave way to fancy dresses in spring colors that coordinated with shoes and bags and hair bows.

The bustling and jostling were breathless, but good-natured. As each completed her look, she shot out the door like a bride late for her own wedding, pausing only for hugs-and-kisses goodbyes to everybody. When the air cleared from the clouds of perfume, Jesus was the only child left in the house.

He carried his specialness without undue arrogance, but they all knew that he was the one Porfirio had longed for through five pregnancies. The girls were beloved by their father; after they left, Porfirio showed me the oversized pictures of each that were hanging on the walls. But they were girls. Jesus was proof of Porfirio's manhood, and manhood meant everything to Porfirio, who excused himself and went out shortly after the girls left. No one expected him to show up at church.

Artemia, who had been making tamales at Doña Sole's all day, was back in the kitchen. Sixto and I offered to help as she began preparations for dinner. The space was small and her cooking technique was efficient and practiced. She didn't want our assistance, just our company. What she wanted was to talk—and she did so with the speed and urgency of someone who is rarely listened to.

I didn't understand much more than the periodic laments of "¡Ah, Sixtito!" that she used to punctuate her monologue. When she said that, Sixto would murmur some affirmation, and she'd go right on. He rarely had a chance to interject anything, and it just didn't seem like the right time for me to point out that I couldn't understand a word she was saying. Artemia had a dignity that transcended Porfirio's bluster. But that night she was in dire need of talk therapy, and Sixto was her therapist.

By the time dinner was ready, the family was back. The girls set the table and showed us to our places. They brought us water and coffee as we all squeezed around the table with Porfirio at the head. All except Artemia. There was no place set for her at the table. She didn't need one.

There is an expression in Mexico that people sometimes use when being introduced. They say their name and add, *para servirle*. It means: I am here to serve you. It isn't just used by the concierge in a fancy hotel. I've had women tell me that when I enter their homes. It was Artemia's motto. She was there to serve us. Literally.

She roamed from the kitchen to the table bringing the meal and attending to our needs. When she wasn't in motion, she was standing behind Porfirio's chair, doting on him and making sure he didn't have to reach too far for a tortilla. He ignored her for the most part, accepting it all as his due. A lion in his pride.

The meal was royal fare: *albondigas*—a meatball dish flavored with mint. Artemia's version was rich beyond description.

"*Invento yo*," she told me as she ladled it into my bowl. I invented this.

There were also beans, of course, the lovely yellow Mayocoba beans that are more delicate to the taste and the digestive system than the more common pintos. Artemia had also made tortillas, fried potatoes, and carne cooked with chile and onions. Porfirio kept urging me to eat more. Sixto kept urging Artemia to come and sit down.

When he was done, Porfirio pushed back his chair and announced grandly: "*Lo demas para las mujeres*." Which translates as: What's left is for the women.

Porfirio went to rest on the couch, clearly expecting Sixto to join him. Sixto helped us clear the table and do the dishes—over the protests of both Artemia and Porfirio.

It was hard to get too mad at Porfirio. His self-image was as carefully crafted as the silver ornamentation on a vaquero's dress saddle—and just as fastidiously polished. He'd always done things his own way, whether it was good for him or not.

When he was young, his older sister would push him through the school door and he'd be out the window before she could turn around. He refused to learn to read—despite the admonitions of his parents and siblings. When their nagging got to be too much, he went to live with another family across the canal. He was only seen at school again when he returned as the driver of a big piece of earth-moving equipment. He handled it well. He found a way to make a living that was more in keeping with his image of a man than wrestling with reading and writing. He knew enough arithmetic to keep Artemia on a tight budget, and lived his vision of a man's life in the city.

In his fantasies, he was the patron of a fine ranch like the one where Artemia grew up. He wanted cows that his wife could milk, horses for his son to ride, and cattle for him to take to market and sell for big profits. Artemia would help him realize the more realistic parts of that dream long after their children were grown. But for now, he had a miniature—and exquisitely detailed—saddle hanging from the mirror of his pickup. His key chain was in the shape of a tiny cow hoof, and it was covered in real cowhide. His handle on the CB radio that he and Artemia used to communicate when he was on the road was "Vaquero."

Porfirio was snoring when we finished the dishes. The girls put the chairs on the table and swept and mopped the floor. Artemia brought a blanket for Porfirio. He'd sleep on the couch that night. She'd sleep with the girls. They had already put our bags in the room she shared with Porfirio. We were to have their bed. Neither one of them would listen to our protests about not wanting to inconvenience them. We were honored guests. Our only option was to acccept.

Porfirio went out early the next morning and bought fish for Artemia to cook for breakfast. He took me into the kitchen so I could see how fresh the fish were as they floated in water in a white plastic bucket. Artemia would cook them just right, he told me. And just in case I didn't like fish, Artemia sent one of the girls to the store to bring back a box of cornflakes. There were also beans, fresh tortillas, fried potatoes, and eggs on the table as Artemia served us that morning. And instant coffee.

The flight home was blissfully uneventful. We passed through US customs after declaring our suitcases were full of tamales and cookies, and emerged to find my mother waiting to drive us home. We sat around our kitchen table, which was wood, not Formica like Doña Sole's. It would have glistened just like hers if we'd kneaded lard into its surface. Of course, we didn't. Lard wasn't good for you. On this side of the border, we all knew that. On those rare occasions when we made tamales, we used vegetable shortening.

I was glad to be home with my bright counters and sparkling sinks. I felt enormous gratitude in knowing there was a full bathroom just down the hall, and that Sixto and I would share our own bed that night.

We unpacked the tamales and cookies that had been designated specially for my mother, and told her how much Doña Sole had enjoyed the candy dish she sent down. As we filled her in on the news of in-laws she'd never met, she asked when Sixto's mother was going to come to visit.

"It would be easier for you to go down there," Sixto said. "It's hard to get a visa."

This is how our next big journey started.

CHAPTER ELEVEN

Over Thanksgiving dinner 1990, my mother and my sister and her son decided they would come with us to meet Sixto's family. The plans included flying into Los Mochis, staying a few days at Doña Sole's, and then taking the train down into Copper Canyon. We would leave right after Christmas.

As soon as it was decided, my mother starting wondering what gift she should take for Sixto's mother. After some discussion, she settled on a purse. It was personal, but not too personal. It was useful, but it didn't imply that Sixto's mother was needy. My mother didn't want to appear to be arriving from the United States with an armload of charity; I was the one with the Lady Bountiful complex.

We went shopping together and she bought a purse for Doña Sole that cost far more than she would have spent on herself. That part of the gift was known only to me—she would never say anything about the cost to Sixto. She sorted through her change for a couple of days until she found a shiny new penny to put in the purse. This, she said, was for luck. It would assure the purse would never be without money. She wrote up an explanation of this good-luck superstition, and asked Sixto to translate it into Spanish so she could put a note in the purse with the penny.

Sixto was reluctant.

This was odd because he was usually enthusiastic about doing anything my mother asked him to do. He tried to dismiss the idea, in his cheerful way, by saying it wasn't necessary; his mother would be thrilled enough to get the purse. He tried to change the subject. My mother stayed on task. She put the paper with what she'd written on the table in front of him, along with a blank sheet for him to write out the Spanish version. She'd type out the translation on her computer and print it out on some pretty paper she bought just for the occasion. She showed Sixto the paper; it had flowers around the edge.

Still, Sixto resisted.

It is my husband's nature to talk around a subject before he gets to the point, but this time he seemed particularly reluctant to explain himself clearly. They went 'round and 'round in a friendly way. My mother was relentless. Eventually Sixto explained: his mother was illiterate. She wouldn't be able to read the note, he told my mother. His expression begged her not to think less of him. I tried to hide my own astonishment. This had never occurred to me.

My mother didn't show any reaction.

"Then you can read it to her," she told him with a shrug, tapping the page she wanted translated.

Her gift was going to include a penny and an explanation. This was not negotiable. If Sixto had to read the note to his mother, so be it. No big deal.

Sixto did the translation while my mother put the kettle on for some tea.

During the weeks of preparation for our trip, I tried to consider every possible contingency and plan for it. Most importantly, I shopped for clothes that would be as elegant as those the women on the Mexican side of my family would be wearing. No more country bumpkin. In addition to looking good, the clothes had to accent my pregnancy.

Yes, Manuel, I had the Egyptian disease.

I made sure everything I wore showed off every millimeter of my expanding belly. I also made sure I had matching shoes and other suitable accessories. I was going to look good this time. I, too, could be elegant without the aid of plumbing, mirrors, or decent lighting. It just took a little planning.

My mother wondered if she should take her "space blankets," metallic sheets that folded up smaller than a deck of cards and were guaranteed to keep you warm on the surface of the moon. She'd gotten them as a free gift with mail-order vitamins. I thought it was silly, but I said sure, take them along. There were also other gifts to be considered. Sixto wanted to take practical stuff again, like sheets and towels. I wanted something more interesting, like serving dishes, lace tablecloths, and, of course, a blender. He insisted people could always use sheets and towels, so we took those, too.

My sister's husband was not coming on the trip. It would be just the five of us. My mother, sister Patty, and her son Devon were bright-eyed and eager as we left for the airport.

"Are you ready for the big adventure?" I asked my nephew Devon.

As it turned out, none of us were ready.

When we got back, the January 6, 1991, headline on the front page of the *Arizona Daily Star* announced: "Homes swept away—Floodwaters wreak devastation in Sinaloan towns; death toll is 5." The story told of the worst flood in local memory. In some towns, only the roofs of houses were visible above the floodwaters. At least 27,000 people were being fed in relief shelters, but that didn't count all of those who had evacuated themselves to higher ground or those who were stranded on their own rooftops in remote communities that were cut off by downed bridges and washed-out roads.

Nor did the news coverage tell of the little band of gringos who sought refuge on a small hill in the middle of some of the 150,000 acres of crops that were destroyed by that flood.

That was us. We went to Mexico on vacation and became part of a news story.

CHAPTER TWELVE

It started like a scene out of an old movie. We exited the plane in Los Mochis down a set of portable stairs onto the tarmac. A crowd of people was pressed up against a fence outside the airport's lone building. A cluster of them erupted into shouts and waves when Sixto and I emerged from the plane. This time Sixto held my purse as well as the carry-ons. My job was to hold the railing and move slowly. This was actually my second pregnancy; the first ended in a miscarriage, though neither of us spoke about that.

As we entered the building, a large contingent of Sixto's family surrounded us.

The protocol was instantly clear: matriarchs ruled.

Everyone waited as Sixto's mother hugged him and wept. Then she hugged me and wept. Then the mothers-in-law were introduced and Sixto translated their words of greeting as others watched respectfully. Then my sister and nephew were introduced to his mother, and Sixto translated their words of greeting. After that, it was largely a free-for-all of hugs, kisses, air kisses, handclasps, laughter, and salutations.

"*Somos muchos*," Toñita said. We are many. They all seemed eager to get even bigger by adding a few North Americans.

A great deal of attention was paid to my pregnant belly. I was only sorry Manuel wasn't there to congratulate us. But he and Ana were living in Ciudad Obregón, and he had duties at the church where he preached. They would travel to Los Suárez later in the week.

Sixto and some nephews went to get our luggage as the rest of us made our way, like some giant, bilingual amoeba, toward the big glass doors that led to the parking lot. Trini brought around the truck, and Toñita gave us directions. La Señora, my mother, would ride up front with her and Doña Sole. There was room, they insisted, for me to sit up front, too. Ordinarily, my sister would have been given that honor because she was older. But I was pregnant and that was a trump card. It would have been a tight squeeze, so I decided to ride in the camper shell with the others.

The drive to Los Mochis was a pageant of rural Mexico. On one side of the road there were little houses peeking out from under mounds of fuchsia, neon-orange, or cranberry-red bougainvillea. The other side of the road was lined with tremendous cottonwood trees that marked the edge of fields of sorghum. Under the trees there was commerce and conversation. Shelves of wooden kiosks were stacked with cans of motor oil. A man pedaled a tricycle-cart that had a frozen-fruit bar painted on the side. A woman shaved *raspados* from a huge block of ice set on the tailgate of a pickup truck. A boy waved a sign announcing that the once-white plastic ice chest he was sitting on was full of *camarones*—shrimp. Men with nothing to sell sipped from bottles they kept in paper bags. Women and children walked to the bus stop.

Through the window of the camper, I could see conversation in the cab of the truck that looked as lively as the scene outside. My mother didn't speak Spanish, and none of them spoke English, but they were laughing and gesturing.

The mood where we were was more somber. Sixto was listening quietly to something one of Toñita's sons was telling him. When I asked what was wrong, he said: "Nothing, mi amor."

But he didn't sound convincing.

We drove for about thirty minutes, then did a U-turn. As we headed back the way we'd come, Sixto slid opened the window to the cab. Trini told him the road was out, but not to worry. He knew another way. A few more miles, a few more turns, and he stopped again, this time by the side of the road.

The men got out and talked. When Sixto got back in, he explained that there had been some trouble upstream on the Rio

Fuerte. Runoff from too much rain was threatening the dam, and the government had ordered a release of water. The dam was miles upstream, but the Rio Fuerte around Los Mochis was rising fast. There was talk of releasing more water, which could create real problems for the low-lying areas—like Los Suárez and Cohui bampo. So far, one bridge was closed, and another was iffy.

Trini figured out a third option, Sixto explained. It would take a little longer, but we'd be fine.

"Did you tell my mother?" I asked.

Sixto opened the little window to the cab and told her what was going on.

"I know," she said, "your mother explained it to me."

How this had been accomplished was beyond me.

It was nearly dark when we arrived at Doña Sole's house. The truck pulled in under the avocado tree, and relatives and neighbors flowed out of the house, which now had glass windows and a sturdy metal front door. It was open, of course.

Doña Sole kept my mother at her side and introduced her to everyone—not by her name, but by her place in the family. She was the mother of Doña Sole's son's wife. She was an instant and honored member of the matriarchs' club. Tía Chayo, who'd been there all day to help with the cooking, wept and hugged us all with great joy, pausing to wipe her face with a towel she had over her shoulder. Doña Mariyita also wiped her eyes with her towel as she greeted Sixto and me and welcomed the newcomers.

Before we were even in the house, a group of children ran out to hand us each a glass of water.

"Wait, mi amor," Sixto said.

He asked whether it was purified water, and the chain of questioning went back to the kitchen. Yes, they got it from the big bottle. Then Sixto asked his mother if that bottle was purified water. Doña Sole didn't exactly roll her eyes, but she made it clear that he was overreacting.

"*Si, si. Agua purificada,*" she said in a slightly exasperated tone.

She knew she had guests with special needs. She'd been getting ready for weeks.

We made our way past a houseful of people—honestly, I didn't recognize them all—to the heart of the house: the kitchen.

Preparations for our arrival had been underway all day. Outside the back door, a pan of beans was slowly cooking over mesquite coals. Inside, the little stove was weighted down by a huge pot of something that smelled amazing—rich and meaty. Two of the four butane-powered burners were covered with a black rectangular *comal* on which Nelly was making tortillas. She cooked them two at a time, turning them by hand and plopping them onto a towel when they were done. Next to that towel, the cutting table was covered with onion skins, carrot tops, and the remains of all sorts of other chopping and slicing.

Two nephews rushed in to ask where to put our suitcases. This led to a great deal of discussion about options and protocol.

The old mud house in back had been taken down after Luis crossed the line to live in Los Angeles. Emilia had moved to a house with an older man who had four children by a previous marriage, and a brand-new, six-month-old child by Emilia. Little Anayetzi also lived with them. That left an empty bedroom in Doña Sole's house.

It had a small bed. The three folded cots leaning up against the wall behind the bed would not fit in the room once they were opened up. But they could easily be set up in the living room after dinner was over and the table was pushed out of the way. We were happy to divvy up that space.

But as the suitcases were being moved onto the bed in the spare room, Doña Sole said my mother's things should be placed in her room. My mother was to have her bed; she would sleep on a cot. Once this was translated, my mother vigorously protested. Sixto performed the duties of mediator and translator as the two matriarchs held their ground. Both were stubborn, and he was trying hard not to offend either one of them. Eventually, they agreed to share the bed.

Sixto and I were assigned to the bed in Emilia's old room. Folding cots would be set up for my sister and Devon in the living room.

But first, there was all that food to eat.

Beef stewed with chiles, tomatoes, potatoes, carrots, green beans, and pieces of sweet corn still on the cob. It tasted more complex than the simplicity of its ingredients. There were little green lemons to squeeze on top, adding a zesty touch. Nelly brought us tortillas hot off the comal, not bothering to serve the ones she'd been cooking and piling on the kitchen towel. There were beans, too, the lovely Mayocoba beans that I remembered from my last visit.

Tía Chayo bustled around with Doña Sole treating us like visiting royalty. No matter how hard we tried to get up from the table so that some of the others could sit down to eat, Doña Sole or Tía Chayo insisted we keep our seats and eat more—or at the very least have hot water for tea. They remembered my fondness for tea. What's more, my mother, forewarned about the instant coffee, brought her own box of Lipton tea, from which my sister and I intended to poach.

The front door was open, and people came and went, gathering around the table and joining in the conversation.

After dinner we made halfhearted offers to wash the dishes, but were easily convinced to leave them on the table outside until morning.

It wasn't late, but the sun had long been down, and it was long past bedtime in this ejido. Toñita left to catch the bus, and others drifted home.

The sky was full of stars when my mother and I were brushing our teeth in the front yard. Trini returned to give us a fuzzy blanket that had a picture of a tiger slinking through tall grass. After final goodnights, Doña Sole locked the doors and turned out the lights.

I had only been asleep for a short time when I heard the knocking. Doña Sole went to the front door and opened a little window to see who was out there.

Sixto was already sitting on the edge of the bed, pulling on his shoes, when she came to get him. They went outside, closing the door quietly behind them.

Roosters were crowing. That wasn't unusual. They often sang all night when the moon was full. But I could also hear voices in the distance and the sound of car doors slamming and engines idling. This was unusual. The nights were always quiet in Los Suárez, except for an occasional truck on the main road.

Sixto and Doña Sole came back in. I heard her slide the metal bolt on the door. Sixto came back to bed.

"Go to sleep, mi amor," he said, "everything is fine."

It was the second time he'd said that. I knew him well enough to know he was saying what he hoped was true.

A few minutes later, someone once again tapped on Doña Sole's metal front door. Once again, I heard her pad across the floor and open the little window. This time Sixto didn't wait for her to call him. They went outside. When they returned, Doña Sole did not shut the door. She turned on the lightbulb in the kitchen.

Sixto very calmly told us that we all had to get up and leave the house. The river was rising too fast. Nobody knew how high the water would go. Just to be safe, we'd wait it out on a small hill about a half a mile behind the house. We dutifully began to get dressed. We were sleepy, and inconvenience had not yet turned to anxiety. It was hard to imagine a flood could do us much harm; it wasn't even raining.

Doña Sole, on the other hand, was moving with great determination. She started packing up food and piling it in front of the house, along with bottles of purified water.

Emilia drove up in a truck driven by Chalino, the father of her second child. He had lost one hand and forearm in an accident years ago, but it didn't slow him down as he helped Sixto and Trini put much of Doña Sole's furniture on the roof of the house. We consolidated a few things into one suitcase, and put it with the supplies that Doña Sole had been amassing in front of the house. Sixto stashed our other suitcases on the roof.

Then they started loading the truck. Doña Sole disconnected the stove from the butane tank and the men loaded both into the truck, too.

"How long are we going to be up there?" my mother asked.

Nobody answered.

We squeezed into the bed of the truck, and Trini, Nelly, and their three boys joined us. Sixto noted with disapproval that Emilia did not offer my mother or her own mother the place of honor in the front of the truck. Even at a time like this, Sixto thought it was important to show respect for the mothers.

Chalino drove through the cropland toward a hill that didn't look big enough to host a Valdez family reunion, let alone this entire ejido. He got as high as possible, past some of the other trucks parked at the base of the hill. Before he had turned off the engine, Doña Sole was out of the truck and moving quickly up a rocky path. She found a good spot at the top, and told the men to set up the stove there. Lots of people were arriving and the flat places were going fast.

When everything was unloaded, Trini, Sixto, and Chalino went back to get some cots and some blankets. Devon went with them.

The dawn was milky by then, and from the little hill we could see what was happening.

The irrigation canal on the other side of the main road was beginning to overflow its concrete embankment and spread across the road toward Doña Sole's house. We couldn't see her house; most of the houses in the ejido were hidden under a canopy of mango and avocado trees. But we could see where the water was headed. In a short time, it would be lapping at Doña Sole's front door.

Somewhere upstream, the Rio Fuerte must have also jumped its banks. The road between Cohuibampo and Los Suárez was shimmering with water as the sun rose. This flow, too, was headed for Los Suárez.

Inconvenience turned into anxiety as we watched.

Nobody knew if our little hill would turn into an island or disappear under water.

After the men got back with the cots, Sixto set them up so we'd have a place to sit. He'd also brought his mother's machete, and he used it to whack off some tree branches and shape them into poles for a tent. He worked with elegance and confidence as he made a shelter for our family. Trini helped.

They wanted to make another trip back to pick up some plastic tarps to finish the tent. Trucks continued to arrive with loads of people and possessions, so the road through the fields was still passable. But it was iridescent under spreading water, so my sister didn't want Devon to make this trip. But he talked her into it.

We waited on the cots this time, watching the truck head back to the village, against the other traffic.

While we waited, Doña Sole made tortillas. She'd brought

everything she needed, including the comal. She'd also brought beans, cheese, and coffee. Breakfast was ready by the time they got back with the tarps. My mother, sister, and I seemed to be the only ones surprised.

Devon had rescued a dog who'd been trapped on the wrong side of rising water, and he told us all about it as we ate. After breakfast, we sipped instant coffee. If it hadn't been for the rising water and the rest of the village settling in around us, we could have been on a picnic.

Emilia thought of more things she wanted from the house, so Chalino headed back through the rising water one more time. Thankfully, he went alone. Sixto set up a little shade ramada for us so we could watch in comfort as he, Trini, and Devon finished the tent.

Doña Sole handed me Emilia'a baby with the recommendation that I get a little practice. The baby's name was Daniela. She started crying about five seconds after her grandmother walked away. My sister took her off my lap and she stopped crying immediately. That pretty much summed up my skill with babies. I really did need the practice.

But I didn't need a reminder that I was pregnant. Fears about losing the baby lapped at the edges of my mind like rising floodwaters.

Sixto and I took a walk around the hill looking for a distraction.

The evacuation had been voluntary and incremental, so there had been time for people to bring whatever they thought they'd need. There were lots of other structures being built and covered with tarps and old plastic tablecloths. Most people had cots just like ours, but some had mattresses, too. There were lots of stoves and butane tanks, with boxes of pots and pans stacked alongside. There were bottles of water and bags that presumably contained the kinds of staples Doña Sole brought along: flour, lard, ground corn, potatoes, beans, eggs, cheese. Some camps had tables and chairs where the women sat over cups of coffee.

It was an instant village.

Dogs wandered around. Pigs were staked lower on the hill—presumably downwind. The chickens that usually scratched freely throughout the village were tethered by a cord tied to one leg.

They squawked when they reached the end of the line. These were the original free-range chickens, and they deeply resented being leashed.

People greeted us as we passed their camps, and we'd stop to chat. They were cordial with us and uniformly disgusted with the situation their government had created. The more generous ones said the officials should have considered the consequences it would have downstream when they released water from the dam. Most simply assumed the bureaucrats didn't care. What did the inconvenience of the people matter if there was an expensive dam to be saved?

They looked only to God to assure the supply of beans and water lasted until they could go home. Especially water. We would be here for weeks, they said.

Weeks?

If that happened, disease would doom us regardless of how long the beans held out.

I considered the dangers. Cholera. Dysentery. Death.

Sixto said everything would be fine, but my baby did little to reassure me.

She wasn't moving anymore. A few weeks earlier, she'd begun kicking at regular intervals. What's more, each evening, she would hiccup for ten or fifteen minutes. Now she was unusually still.

This gave me an empty, lonely feeling that I didn't want to empower by putting it into words. I was holding Sixto's hand, but it felt like he was on the other side of the world.

Tía Chayo joined us on our walk. Unlike Toñita, she hadn't gone home the night before. She'd stayed with her son in Los Suárez, and now she was stuck on the hill.

Her talkativeness was welcome and reassuring. I didn't even have to hold up my end of the conversation. A nod or a smile would keep her talking in those lullaby cadences. The world could not end while Tía Chayo was talking. Even God wouldn't dare interrupt.

Tía Chayo's salt-and-pepper hair was so thick that her daughters said she sometimes had to sit down to rest her braid on the back of the couch; the weight could give her a headache. I once saw her hair when it was freshly washed. One of her daughters was trying to comb the mane into submission, but it was like a wild creature with a will of its own, undulating irrepressibly. Here on the hill, it was braided into a placid rope that rested on the tiny print of her cotton dress. She had no way of knowing how bad the flooding was around her home in Cohuibampo, or where her family would be able to find high ground.

But Tía Chayo didn't dwell on that. She was very concerned about me. She kept telling Sixto he had to get me out of there, and I couldn't have agreed more.

When we got back to our camp, Tía Chayo joined my mother, who also had salt-and-pepper hair, though hers was short-cropped with bangs that fell above green Irish eyes. My mother's good-mannered attentiveness was easily mistaken by Tía Chayo for comprehension as they sat side-by-side on a cot.

Doña Sole made more tortillas, and we used them to scoop up mashed beans for dinner as the sun set on December 30, 1990. We didn't want to use precious drinking water to wash the pan, so we covered it with the comal to keep out any critters that might come around in the night.

The air picked up a chill as it passed over the dark, flooded fields and we tried to get cozy under the shelter Sixto and Trini had built. Sixto had used my mother's "space blankets" to line our cots so the cold air didn't come up through the burlap during the night. He split the two blankets to make four. My cot, my mother's, and my sister's had a layer of foil that crinkled loudly whenever one of us changed positions. Devon and Sixto were on the ground. Devon got the fourth quarter of the space blanket after Doña Sole declined it. But the noise made him crazy so he wadded it up and wedged it under a rock.

Trini's twin boys were jumping on their cot and laughing. Doña Sole was fast losing her patience with their antics. Her suggestion that Trini "give them some" was illustrated by a hand chopping the air. Trini hung up a blanket between their cots and ours. It was the tiger blanket from the night before, but the way Trini put it up left the cat upside down, like a turtle on its back. It did nothing to stop the noise of the boys. Doña Sole sighed loudly in response to their ever-louder shrieks of laughter, but said nothing more. Emilia and her husband were sleeping in the truck with the little ones. I hadn't seen Chalino's older children since we arrived, but Sixto said they were there.

The roosters started crowing as soon as the moon came up. Dogs wandered around looking for scraps of food, and pigs snuffled. There were a few fires, and people gathered around them to talk softly and laugh.

Nothing was still except my baby.

The next morning was the last day of 1990 and our first full day on the hill. The crops in the fields were invisible under the floodwater that now flowed deep across the road. Nobody was going anywhere. Those who claimed special knowledge of such things said the water had stopped rising. By midday, the evidence was on their side. It licked the base of our hill, but it wasn't climbing up to get us.

My baby was still quiet.

I remembered a Christmas potluck at church. Before we ate, everybody gathered in a huge circle around all the tables in the fellowship hall and sang the "Twelve Days of Christmas." When we were done singing, people began to call out their wishes for the coming year, and then we would all repeat each wish as a prayer. I wanted to shout out: "Here's to all the babies who will be born in 1991!" But I was too timid in those days to speak up in a crowd. The words circled around in my head, but I never spoke them. Now they were circling my head again, making me feel guilty and afraid. I wished I had asked all those people to pray for my baby. I needed those prayers now. My baby needed them. What if I lost her on this hill? These thoughts prowled like jackals in my brain, ready to devour any sense of well-being that might creep in. Ready to damn me for this unforgivable sin of omission.

Doña Sole was frying beans.

"I could sure use a cup of tea right now," my mother said. She was never a coffee drinker. Her box of tea was in her suitcase on the roof of Doña Sole's house.

"I'm really sick of hearing about tea," snapped one of the jackals in my head. I regretted the words the minute I heard myself say them. This was the first time she'd mentioned tea.

"Well, I'm sick of hearing about all the things you are complaining about," she hissed back. This, too, was unjustified. I hadn't been complaining, just simmering in my silent fears.

We fell silent. Sixto said he'd ask around to see if anybody brought tea to the hill. My mother patted his arm and told him not to worry. She said she was happy to have the coffee his mother brought.

It was delicious, she said.

He shot me a look that made me feel even worse.

I wanted to cry out that this wasn't about tea. What mattered was that her granddaughter-to-be hadn't moved for more than a day, and that it was probably all my fault for not speaking up in church at Christmas. But I said nothing. For the rest of the day, my mother and I tippy-toed around each other's feelings. Neither of us was able to offer the comfort we both needed.

The other people on the hill were surprisingly upbeat as they looked down on this catastrophe engulfing their lives. It was obvious from the water level across the fields that the flood must be flowing through everybody's homes. We just didn't know how high.

Doña Sole's had a new refrigerator. A tiny thing with a single door and a freezer made claustrophobic by walls of lumpy frost. It was her first refrigerator, bought with money we'd sent by Western Union a few months earlier. The men, who had worked without a ladder to get tables, chairs, and beds on the roof, had not moved it. That's when I realized that bringing the stove to the hill was as much about saving a valuable asset as it was about preparing hot meals for us.

It was sunny again that day, which made the whole thing more surreal. I had always imagined floods coming from raging storms and pounding rain. But our disaster was unfolding under a clear blue sky. By midafternoon, the sun was so hot that my mother, sister, and I sat in the shade structure Sixto had built. We did not mention tea or babies.

That night was New Year's Eve, and there was an unlikely air of celebration as a group of men built a big fire near our camp. These guys yelled jolly-sounding comments and Sixto bantered back, but did not join them. Trini also stayed away. They talked louder and laughed more as the night went on. When they began passing around a bottle in a paper bag, Doña Sole snorted in disgust and commented loudly enough for them to hear about the *tontería* of those who remembered to bring liquor when we'd probably all be out of water soon. Emilia tried to shush her and eyed the men's party with interest.

Sixto had been very unhappy when his mother called us in Tucson to say Emilia had moved in with Chalino. There were several problems, as he saw it. Chalino was already married —albeit permanently separated—so he could not marry Emilia. She, too, was also still technically married to Anayetzi's abusive father. Emilia's husband hadn't been heard from in years, but Chalino's wife lived in a nearby village. Her four children were living with Emilia and Chalino, and she had full legal right to make trouble for Emilia at any time.

Chalino seemed to have a genuine fondness for Emilia, and his children treated Emilia with sufficient respect. Doña Sole accepted the arrangement. It was Emilia's little girl, Anayetzi, that Doña Sole worried about. When he and Emilia got together, Chalino welcomed Anayetzi to the family without reservation, but she was not thriving. She was frail and ate little except when her grandmother fed her. Under the moon that New Year's Eve, Anayetzi was cozied down in Doña Sole's lap when Emilia told her to get up and follow them down to the truck. She can sleep here, her grandmother said. Emilia said no, so Anayetzi got up and left.

I was still awake at midnight when the men at the fire began wishing each other *Feliz Año Nuevo*. Salutation could be heard from all parts of the hill. The men near us piled more wood on the fire—another waste in Doña Sole's opinion—and hunkered down to drink in seriousness. By morning, a few of them were still huddled around the warm ashes.

CHAPTER THIRTEEN

In the damp dawn, the matriarchs came by to wish their co-
madre, Doña Sole, and her family a Happy New Year.
We all shook hands, clapped each other on the shoulders, and
wished each other the best in the coming year. This was a remarkable display of goodwill from people whose homes were in ruins.
They were hopeful about 1991.

Who knew? It could be a great year.

I silently wished the best for all the babies who would be born
that year. Mine was still not moving.

Our tent city was peaceful and orderly. People respected each
other's space, and even the men who drank by the fires at night
remained civil and well within the social restraints that demand-
ed cordial and polite treatment of women and kind attentiveness
toward other people's children.

No one was in charge and no group stepped up to establish
community rules. It didn't matter except in the one area: sanitation. From the first day, people had simply found a private place
to relieve themselves. Certain places had natural appeal because
rocks or vegetation provided cover. These areas quickly became
overwhelmed with waste, so people shifted to different locations. Some people dug holes and tried to bury the mess, but this
was complicated because you never knew who had buried what
where. Most folks just tried to hide themselves as they heeded
nature's call. As a result, parts of that little hill were becoming
toxic and when the wind shifted, the smell was bad.

It was just a matter of time before the weight of so many people would overwhelm a pretty little hill that previously had been dominated by black rocks and columnar cactus.

Chalino's truck didn't have a working radio, but one of the vehicles parked at the other side of the hill did. News began to circulate about the extent of the flood, and people discussed what this meant for relatives. There was no specific news about Cohui bampo, which was lower and closer to the river than Los Suárez. Tía Chayo and Doña Sole wept into their towels and prayed for Toñita and her family and Tía Chayo's family as they made tortillas. Sixto asked if they were going to salt the tortillas with tears. Doña Sole waved her towel at him, and they laughed.

Then they turned their attention to me.

Tía Chayo's concern about my condition expanded to include my American family. We weren't used to such conditions, she told Sixto, and things were going to get worse. He had to get us out of there. The radio newscasters had mentioned military helicopters that had been dispatched to rescue people. If they came by, she said, we needed to wave them down and make sure they took me, my mother, my sister, and Devon. We weren't used to living like this, she repeated.

Of course, Tía Chayo wasn't used to living like that, either. None of them were. They might be poor people, but they had a level of order and sanitation in their homes that was impossible to achieve here. Nevertheless, Tía Chayo was preoccupied with me and mine.

Later that day, a helicopter did fly over our hill. People waved and shouted and jumped up and down. But it kept going.

People returned to stoves or chairs or cots or rocks, feeling less comfortable now that a hint of rescue had passed them by.

About an hour later, people started yelling again. The chopper was back. It circled our island-hill as people screamed and waved their arms. After a few more passes, it hovered over a small, quarried area at the back of the hill. It was relatively flat, but nobody had camped there because it was covered in small, sharp rocks. Once it became clear the helicopter was going to land, Doña Sole and Tía Chayo whipped us into action. We had to get over there, they told Sixto.

A crowd surrounded the quarry by the time the helicopter set down. Mouths were moving and arms were pumping, but the pounding of the helicopter's blades was the only sound you could hear. When the engine stopped, the yells of hundreds of desperate people filled the air. Rescue me. Bring us beans. We need water.

There was a sudden sense of panic among people who were happily wishing each other Happy New Year a few hours earlier. Everybody wanted on that helicopter.

A couple of federales got out and motioned people to stay back. They had big guns.

One young soldier stepped forward, his weapon at the ready. People began to advance. He waved them back. One man was permitted to step forward and talk to the officer. Those who were close enough to hear relayed the important parts of the conversation.

The soldiers had brought nothing. No food. No water. No news about how long it would be before the flood receded. They were authorized to take anyone off the hill who was sick or in particular need.

Tía Chayo shoved me forward. Sixto pulled me back.

Then an even more pregnant woman waddled forward. I had not seen her before. Looking ready to deliver at any instant, she moved slowly and held a child of three or four by the hand. The young soldier with the oversized gun nodded toward the helicopter, and the woman began to pick her way over the rough gravel toward it. You could feel the crowd's collective assent. These idiots had not brought supplies or useful information, but at least they had the good sense to help this woman and her little girl. Word spread through the crowd that she was from another village; her husband was not with her.

Before she got to the helicopter, another soldier got out and spoke to her. We could see her shake her head vigorously as the little girl began to cry. Another murmur spread through the crowd: they wanted her to leave the child behind. The mother kept shaking her head and the little girl cried louder as the young soldier tried to step in and separate them. The woman shook her head again and pulled her child with her back into the waiting crowd. The crowd closed around her. The soldiers shrugged.

Was there no one else? A family came forward with a sick old

man. He'd been fainting, they said. They didn't know what was
wrong, but they thought he needed to go to a hospital. The soldiers loaded him onto the helicopter and told the family they'd
have to stay behind. Suddenly, this fragile old man's family looked
very sorry for what they had done. Who would take care of him?
He'd be taken care of, the soldier said. But Sixto hissed at us that
the old man was unlikely to get much attention at any hospital
without family members there to plead his case. Sixto and my
mother were clucking about the old man's prospects when Tía
Chayo pushed forward.

She wore her air of grandmotherly authority like armor. Only
a fool would mess with her. She called the soldier "mijo" as she
spoke rapid-fire and gestured at our little band of gringos. He
looked at us and shook his head. She continued talking, determined to get us on that helicopter. Even after Sixto went to gently
usher her back to where we were standing, she continued arguing
that we should be airlifted to comfort and safety.

The helicopter shuddered and wobbled as it rose into the sky,
then it thudded away.

People wandered back to their camps, chewing over the story
of the pregnant woman and her little girl and speculating about
what would become of the old man.

Now that the promised rescue was revealed as an illusion, we
all had to face facts. This hill was our whole world until we found
our own way out, and things were bound to get worse. Nobody
believed the soldiers' promise to return with food and water.

It was a glum afternoon as we sat around once more, watching the flood ripple gently where rows of plants were supposed
to be. But that evening, we saw a glimmer of hope. As the setting
sunlight sliced across the flooded fields, you could see the tops of
a few plants breaking the surface.

The water was receding.

Sixto and Trini were talking quietly as I fell asleep.

The next morning, Sixto explained their plan: we would walk
out that morning.

Trini would come along to help, but Doña Sole, Tía Chayo,
and the rest of the family would wait on the hill. There was no
hope that the water had receded enough for them to go back to

their homes, and they wanted to be close by when it did. Our aim was to get to Los Mochis, which was not flooded, and return with water and supplies. Trini would go with us as far as Cohuibampo and bring back news of the families there.

Doña Sole made tortillas and beans and used some of her dwindling water supply to make coffee, even though we said we didn't need it.

Then we said our goodbyes.

This was a lot more real than running toward a helicopter in the hope of being lifted above it all. This was walking away from people who helped keep us warm, fed, and safe. Sixto said the best thing we could do was bring them what they'd need to stay healthy until they could go back home. But as we made our way down the path that led off the hill, I felt the weight of deserting family and friends.

I was knee deep in standing water as we started down the dirt road on which Chalino had driven us to the hill. Sixto told me to keep my sneakers on because there could be broken glass or other hazards on the road. I had my pants rolled up to my thighs. Trini made a comment to Sixto about how white my legs were. In the United States, this would have been a not-so-subtle suggestion that I was no California girl. But Trini said it with admiration.

It was slow going down that road. It wasn't just the possibility of glass we had to worry about. We had to be sure the road itself had not been washed away. Sixto and Trini stayed ahead, creating a safe path for us to follow.

We found Doña Sole's house still standing in several feet of water, with the high-water mark just below the roofline. Sixto and Trini climbed up to the roof to get our suitcases without saying a word. They walked around the perimeter of the roof of their mother's house, stomping their feet and looking for signs of weakness. I peered in a window and saw a shoe floating in the dirty water. The warm greetings that had been wrapped in delicious smells of dinner, the laughter and the hugs that drew us into this little house were like ghosts, drowned by dirty water.

We all murmured our regrets like little prayers.

The water had retreated from the main road, except for the craters where the pavement was washed out. We could easily walk around this damage, but vehicles would have a tough time navigating the remaining good pavement. Besides, as Sixto pointed out, there was no way of telling just how solid the remaining pavement was. He warned us to stay safely away from the edge of the newly eroded asphalt canyons and road craters.

On the far side of the road, the irrigation canal was once again contained within its concrete lips. But only barely. The water was an ugly tongue licking the edges rhythmically. The current was wicked. As we watched, a dead cow went by, bobbing in the foamy brown water with its stiff legs jutting out.

We didn't see anybody as we began walking toward Cohui bampo.

We passed deserted houses standing in dirty water, with dark stains showing how much worse it had been. How would anyone even begin to clean the rough adobe and porous concrete of those houses? How would you get the smell and germs of outhouses and dead cows out of the walls? Doña Sole and the others faced an enormous job. Before they could even get to it, they had to endure many more long days on that hill, which was descending not into anarchy—people were civil and respectful even under these circumstances—but into environmental collapse. I could almost hear the germs growing when we left.

We walked along, with the irrigation ditch roiling just to the right and flooded houses to our left. We were the first to see the devastation: the pioneers in a newly ruined world.

Old-school manners still governed our Mexican hosts.

Sixto carried his suitcases and mine. Trini had my mother's and one of my sister's. Devon and my sister carried what was left. My mother and I had only our purses because she was a matriarch, and I was pregnant.

My sneakers were gritty from the muddy water, and they were turning to sandpaper as they dried. I sat on the road to take them off, announcing I would rather walk barefoot. Trini instantly kicked off the plastic flip-flops he was wearing and put them in front of me. They were too big, so they made exaggerated slapping sounds as we got moving again. But they were softer than the roadway.

After a while, the drowning houses of Los Suárez gave way

to flooded fields as we walked on. The only sound was the hiss of the irrigation canal. There was no wind under that sunny sky, and none of the usual bustle. No old men on bicycles, no horses tethered near the road to graze on weeds, no cars, no buses, no trucks pushing their engines for speed between the ejidos, no carts. We strained to see something in the road ahead, and finally we did.

There was movement up there. Two figures. Too small for cars, too fast for pedestrians. They were headed toward us. We walked a little faster.

As they got closer, we could see two boys on bicycles. As they got closer still, Sixto and Trini called out to them by name. They skidded to a halt as they reached us and dropped their bikes on the road. The conversation was too fast for me to follow. I heard snippets of "Toñita" and "Cohuibampo" and "*iglesia.*" Sixto and Trini were overjoyed to see them.

They piled our suitcases on the handlebars of the bikes, and the boys rode off.

"We'll never see them again," my sister said. It was her first dire pronouncement, and entirely out of character. She was never one to buy into stereotypes about Mexicans. Our days on the hill must have gotten to her, too.

"At least we don't have to carry that stuff anymore," she added.

Sixto looked surprised.

He thought we'd all recognized Toñita's sons. They'd taken their bikes with them when the family evacuated to the roof of the church. Now they were out in search of news about their mother and Tía Chayo, which Sixto and Trini happily provided.

They also brought news. Good news. They told Sixto the bridge across the Rio Fuerte to Los Mochis was open, though there was talk of closing it soon. Now that the water had receded from the roadway, many who could get their cars to run were heading to the city while they still could. The boys said that road to Mochis was still in pretty good shape, too.

We walked faster then, sensing the promise of a way out.

As we neared Cohuibampo, we passed houses standing in water nearly up to their roofs. People here were camped out on top of their houses, along with furniture and piles of household goods and clothing that they had saved.

When we finished our long walk, we found the boys sitting on our suitcases at a gas station where the road we were on intersected with the road to Mochis. The high-water mark was halfway up the wall of the concrete structure, but this corner was high and the water had subsided entirely. Waterlogged signs offered ice and snacks.

We were standing there considering our options when a car pulled in, looking for gas. Sixto told them the place was closed. They exchanged polite greetings, and it turned out the guy behind the wheel was a distant cousin of somebody Sixto knew. Just like that, we had a ride.

We said goodbye to Trini and the boys, and climbed in: four of us in the back, Sixto in the front. The car was tan and white, an American model from the days when cars were low, long, and rectangular. If the gas held out and the bridge held out, we would be in Mochis in an hour.

Sixto told Trini to tell their mother that he'd be back with water and food before sunset.

The canal had been an ugly hissing presence along the side of the road as we walked. We crossed it now on a bridge that looked sturdy and slotted into thick traffic headed toward the big bridge over the Rio Fuerte.

The line of traffic was moving, but it wasn't moving fast enough for our driver. My sister later said he must have been running toward a happy lover or running away from an unhappy one. Either way, he was highly motivated.

He ran off the road and bumped past traffic on the rutted shoulder. Just as the shoulder was about to disappear into a ditch, he punched the gas pedal and shoved his way between cars on the crowded road. This guy could play chicken with Porfirio, and that was saying something.

When the shoulder reappeared, he cut over and raced along too fast for that old car's shocks to keep up. When necessary, he jumped back on the road. The only sounds were the growling engine and an ominous thumping from somewhere under the car.

Nobody spoke.

Now you might think this was alarming—especially since I

was in a heightened state of anxiety about the baby. But this was the perfect antidote to those endless hours of watching the flood-water. We weren't just moving, we were soaring. We were getting somewhere at last. And getting there fast.

Then we got to the bridge.

Traffic on the approach was packed so tight that even our driver knew there was nothing to do but keep his spot and inch along. This was one of the few bridges still open in these parts.

We could hear the river before we saw it. The sound of it drowned out the labored rumble of that car's hot engine. As we got closer, we could see this river was nothing like that disgusting canal in its concrete ditch, slobbering brown foam and carrying dead farm animals.

The Rio Fuerte could not be dismissed simply as a barrier be-tween here and where we wanted to go. It was a force of nature, full of energy and eager to wash away the memory of all the poor, dam-starved years when its power had been used for somebody else's purposes. The Rio Fuerte served no human needs today. It was not a submissive source of irrigation. Or power. Or trans-portation. It was not even the pre-dam playground where Sixto and his siblings used to swim along beaches scrubbed clean by periodic floods. This was not a Sunday-afternoon river.

This was a river remembering. Heaven help the plant, animal, or person that got in the way of the Rio Fuerte's sudden realiza-tion of being a real river again.

The bridge was a poor thing by comparison. Built for quieter times. But it was being held up by something stronger than just steel and concrete. It was standing because of the hopes of those left behind and the promises of those who went in search of sup-plies. That, too, was powerful.

As we inched across the bridge, I could feel the structure shud-der from the force of the rushing water and the weight of all the cars, trucks and human drama it carried. But then I felt some-thing even more powerful.

My baby kicked me.

It was the Miracle of the Rio Fuerte.

It liberated me, just like the release of water had liberated the river from all those years of being under artificial control. I was free of those days of self-imposed silence and unspeakable fear.

Now I could care about my mother's lack of tea and my sister's diminishing number of cigarettes. Now I could think about what we could do for those back on that hill. Now I could worry about something besides that great abyss where pregnancies fail and women are left to wonder what they could have done differently.

We'd survived. Everything was going to be fine.

I had my First-World mojo back.

When we got to the hotel, I joined my mother and sister in urging Sixto to offer our daredevil driver some money. Sixto said that wasn't necessary. When we continued to insist, Sixto said it would be an insult. As a remote part of a very extended family, it was the driver's honor—if not his duty—to help us out. But our little band of gringos was back on familiar ground in front of that comfortable hotel. We thought we knew better.

In this world—our world—people paid for services. Money talks, and it can say "thank you" louder than words. We thought it was the best way to express our appreciation and admiration for the amazing driving skills that had gotten us here. So we pressed Sixto. He was tired, too, so he relented and offered the driver money.

Then we saw our mistake in the eyes of a man we'd seen as our savior. At first, he looked slightly surprised—the way Sixto had looked surprised when he realized we hadn't recognized his sister's boys. Then, as he refused our money, he looked a little hurt. We'd treated him as a servant. I felt bad as he drove away.

But to be honest, I didn't spend much time worrying about his feelings. I had already moved on to my next concern: I was afraid the hotel would be full.

CHAPTER FOURTEEN

The city was crowded, but the hotel had plenty of room. Few of those who fled the flood could afford to stay there. They stayed with relatives or friends. The stores downtown, on the other hand, throbbed with those who, like Sixto, had promised to bring back water and food to friends and family.

We had barely set down our luggage in our room when Sixto was on the phone trying to reach Porfirio. He left a message with Artemia, which took a long time because he had to fill her in on the news from Los Suárez and Cohuibampo. Then he made sure the others were comfortable in their rooms before he headed out to line up the supplies he planned to take back to the hill.

My assignment was to wait for Porfirio to call. It seemed simple enough.

When the phone rang, I made my first mistake.

I said, "Hello."

There was a sigh, followed by loud breathing. Then I heard a muffled voice as a man spoke, not into the receiver, but to someone in the room with him. I knew it was Porfirio. He was telling Artemia I was speaking English to him. He sounded desperate.

I said "hello" again, in my most cheery voice. Surely *hello* is a universal greeting.

Apparently not.

Porfirio came back on the line, speaking too fast for me to follow. I could only make out "Sixto." Of course, I thought, he's asking for Sixto. I can handle this.

"*No está aquí*," I said slowly. He is not here. It didn't get any more basic than that. Even with my accent, that should have been easy to understand.

Porfirio responded with even more rapid-fire Spanish. Again, I could only make out one thing with certainty: "Sixto." This time, the name was bracketed with large question marks.

"No está aquí," I said again, very slowly. If we can just get past this part, I thought, we can work on something more meaningful.

I could hear more muffled side talk as he consulted with Artemia. He came back with something I didn't understand, and I again repeated my phrase. Finally he got it.

"*¿No está Sixto?*" he said. Sixto isn't there?

"Sí," I said. "No está."

"*¿Sí, está?*"

Oh, no.

I started over. Eventually we got back the question "*¿No está Sixto?*" and I correctly answered "No, no está." No, he's not.

We were making progress now.

Then I made my next mistake. I tried to get the information necessary to take a message.

"*¿Está en casa?*" I asked. Are you home?

More excited talking to Artemia.

"*¿Que?*" he said very loudly when he came back on.

"*¿Está en su casa?*" Are you in your home?

I thought this was pretty clear and understandable. Of course I was using the formal pronoun, which was wrong and would have made him think I was talking about somebody else's *casa*. But really. I'd just walked through floodwaters after spending days wondering if my baby was going to survive. The least he could do was respond to my pidgin Spanish.

All he had to do was say "sí" or "no."

Sixto would have understood me. Doña Sole would have understood me. Tía Chayo would have understood me. Artemia would have understood me, if he had just put her on the line. But Porfirio could not understand me for the simple reason that he didn't expect me to speak Spanish. I was undercut by a stereotype, but I kept trying. Eventually he slammed down the phone. By the time Sixto got back, Porfirio and Artemia were in the lobby, demanding to know what room I was in and acting so crazy that the nice young woman behind the desk refused to tell them. The phone call had convinced them I was under duress, and that Sixto was trapped in somebody's house. They'd rushed over to the hotel. When Porfirio told Sixto about our phone call, Sixto was convinced I must be delirious. He ran up the stairs without waiting for the elevator and burst in our door calling, "Mi, amor, what's wrong?"

Porfirio and Artemia were close behind.

Nothing, I replied.

Porfirio hissed a few curses as we sorted things out.

Sixto and Porfirio made several trips to the hill over the next few days. Porfirio managed to get remarkably close, despite the condition of the road. The floodwater was receding steadily, but very slowly, and the danger of getting stuck in the mud was illustrated by a number of other vehicles they saw hopelessly mired. Porfirio agreed to pull a few out, but only the ones he felt were not idiots.

Doña Sole and the others were still on the hill by the time we flew back to Tucson, although they had walked back a few times to assess the situation at home. Many people stayed in their flood camps even after they could begin reclaiming their houses. The hill was a dry place to return after a day of cleaning out muck. After we got home, my sister wired money down for Doña Sole to buy a new refrigerator. My mother sent prayers.

Doña Sole's house was intact, as we'd found it the day Sixto and Trini had checked the roof. She still had a great deal to clean up, but she was one of the lucky ones.

Some people who returned to old-style houses built of cactus ribs and dirt could only comb through the mud looking to salvage anything that could be washed clean. Plates. Pans. Silverware. A lot of things had floated away with the water and were left strewn along the path of the retreating flood. People retrieved what they could. They cleaned what they could. They rebuilt toppled outhouses.

It is tempting to say they began reconstructing their lives, but it was clear from our time on that little hill that the people with whom we were stranded did not see their possessions as defining their lives. They'd lost plenty. But their lives were built around each other, around family and relationships. These are the assets they would use to begin putting their houses back together.

During every subsequent visit, the people who had been on that hill with us would ask about my mother and my sister and her son. They'd reminisce. They'd tell me to give their regards to my family, and I'd say I would do that with great pleasure. They would talk about how much they admired the way we held up under the circumstances. It must have been so hard for us, they'd say. They didn't think Americans were well prepared for adversity. My image of Mexico was also altered by those few days.

Those who made us part of their world on that hill were not all relatives. But they were all people whose nationality and ethnic identity are routinely decried as a threat to the culture, economy, and social structure of the United States. They were all poor people, whose poverty also makes them instantly suspect of being unable to offer anything of value to anybody else. But their ingenuity and generosity kept us fed and safe.

They didn't stop to ask if we deserved their help. They didn't think about whether we had earned it or if we were worthy to receive it. Nobody asked if our visas were in order. They embraced us. Fed us. Wished us happy New Year.

I have often wondered how a family from Los Suárez would be treated in a camp of Arizonans who had been evacuated from homes that were being destroyed. As strangers—like we were—without food, water, useful skills, or a common language, would they be adopted, protected, and made to feel safe and welcome?

It had been a dramatic trip, but there was one more crisis before we arrived home from that trip that we spent on the hill in Mexico.

In the airport at Hermosillo, I started bleeding, and the terror of a miscarriage returned. The baby had been active since waking up as we crossed the Rio Fuerte, so I'd let that fear go. Now it was back.

Like before, I held the fear inside, not wanting to give it power by putting it into words.

When I called the obstetrician to tell him about the blood that started and then stopped, I also told him about the flood and our days on the hill, and about walking out through the dirty water.

The more I told him, the more convinced I was that he would tell me to give up all hope. He listened in his doctor's way—the way that makes you think he's really got fifty other things on his mind.

Then he said: "It's in God's hands now."

CHAPTER FIFTEEN

My relationship with God has been a bit shaky since the suicide of that young man when I was twenty. I made my peace, as they say, and I had a great fondness for Jesus. But I never quite trusted the Old Man again. Not completely.

When I met Sixto, his faith was so solid I just leaned into it.

I share that dependence on my husband's faith with Doña Sole. She told me about it one night when Sixto had stayed behind at the church to talk—*platicando*, she called it. She and I also talked, and I understood her with remarkable clarity.

She had a big picture of her late husband framed on the wall. It was a simple black-and-white photo, probably from an ID of some sort. Somebody had enlarged it for her to poster size. The image was grainy and faded, but even through those flaws I could see a kind-looking man with delicate features. He graced the room with benevolent humility and powerful dignity. His portrait did not try to dominate the room, the way some portraits do.

But his memory was like a deep knowledge that had helped polish the hard dirt of the floor and continued to rise through the feet that walked on that floor now. It animated Doña Sole. It traveled daily with my husband; he was named for his father.

Sixto the son was at the church now—platicando y platicando, as Doña Sole put it, because of Sixto the father-husband. The Mennonite missionaries came to the village when my husband was six or seven (you ask these specific questions and that's the kind of answer you get: six or seven, maybe eight; the specificity comes in details about who said what, who was cooking what, and what family members were doing). His father took the family to see what they had to offer. Sixto the elder had already rejected what the Catholics had to offer.

The family history, which was kept secret from the children for many years, was that Sixto's father had grown up in a town somewhere to the south of Los Mochis. And he had money then.

Sixto's father was fully literate at a time when most people who lived in mud houses weren't. His destiny had not been to labor from sunup to sundown. As a child, he lived with an aunt who was so well-off that the bishop came to dine at their house on a regular basis. As a young man, he showed the traits of stubbornness and pride that he generously passed on to his son. One day, Sixto's father refused to kiss the bishop's ring. The aunt threatened to whip the young man into compliance, so Sixto the elder ran away and never looked back. He was uncomfortable enough about being associated with that past that he waited until my husband was born—the tenth child—before he would allow his wife to pass on his name.

The young man who defied the bishop traveled around for years, doing whatever itinerant young men did in Mexico in those days. He was in his thirties when he arrived in Los Suárez. There he saw a young girl—she was fourteen—and struck up a conversation from the other side of a barrier of tree-high prickly-pear cactuses. Her name was Soledad. At one point, he asked her, "Is it true you are going to be mine?" She giggled. They were married.

Even death didn't keep them apart now.

As his son talked with friends and neighbors at the church, Doña Sole told me she was never afraid. She nodded at the picture. She knew he was watching over her, protecting her and those she loved. She trusted his spirit to keep her from harm, to intercede on her behalf in heaven.

Doña Sole—like many of her relatives and neighbors—used the expression *con la ayuda de Dios* (with the help of God) in ways that sometimes made me queasy.

For example, when we said we were going home the next day, she would respond, "con la ayuda de Dios." It was a blessing and a prayer, but it always made the journey seem a bit more dangerous. Even saying something on the order of "see you in the morning" was liable to be followed with a reminder that it was up to God's mood. If you slept well, it was celebrated by saying "Gracias a Dios."

But as Doña Sole talked about how her late husband would take care of her, it was clear that he was the one she relied on for the practical stuff. God was in charge. You bet. But God could get too busy for the little stuff. It was Sixto's father who would make sure Doña Sole stayed safe and adequately fed.

Sixto's faith is a comforting thing, too.

I am perfectly happy to assign him the role of intermediary.

The sorrows of life—even many stories in the Bible—make God seem like a petty and mean-spirited tyrant to me. But the apparent inconsistencies are easy for Sixto to explain away. His God is good and generous. Sixto can see larger meaning and even benevolence in the Old Testament tales of expulsions, floods, and mass murder.

It was Sixto who believed we'd get the visa in Tijuana. Sixto who believed we'd have a baby. Sixto who built the shelter on the hill during the flood, and Sixto who knew we'd walk out of there safely together. And when I finally told him about the blood and what the doctor had said after we got back from the flood, Sixto said God had brought us together for a reason.

The baby would be fine, he said.

He was right. But even that was so touch-and-go at the end that it took the enormous faith of him and my mother to make it happen.

We'd gone to the birthing classes, practiced the breathing and the exercises. But when labor came, it came in a fast flood. Contractions were a minute apart from the beginning—and they stayed that way all through the night and into the predawn morning when we finally drove to the hospital. At the end of that day, the nurses said it would be about another hour before the baby came. I told Sixto to call my mother and ask her if she wanted to be there.

Then everything stopped.

The baby's blood pressure dropped.

The doctor ordered a cesarean and we went flying into the operating room, Sixto and my mother trailing behind. They let them stand by the wall as they cut the baby out of my body—as they raced to prevent my body from becoming her tomb. I couldn't see her when they pulled her out. I was conscious, but they had erected a tent on my chest to block my view of the action. I could see my mother and Sixto, though, and they offered smiles and nods of encouragement. They were too far away to provide hand-squeezing comfort.

They never let on about what they saw.

My mother told me later—much later—that the baby was all blue—purple-blue—when they lifted her up. But neither Sixto nor my mother showed the horror they must have been imagining at that moment.

They never stopped believing until the baby turned pink. This was the Miracle of the Beautiful Baby Girl.

Sixto went with the nurses when they took Lucy to wash her off and introduce her to what would one day be among her favorite things: garments. He wanted to make sure they didn't switch babies on him.

After awhile, they moved me into a quiet room. My mother left. Sixto was still with the baby. I was alone. I wanted to sleep. Then a nurse bounded in and handed me a bundle and a few breast-feeding instructions.

Can't this wait till morning, I thought. But I'd moved beyond the luxury of waiting. I was a mother. Now it was all about doing.

From the beginning, though, Sixto was the one who did the heavy lifting. I did the nursing—every two hours, all day. He carried her during the six to eight hours of colic the rest of the day. At night, she slept.

In fact, she slept all night, every night from the day we brought her home from the hospital. She slept so well at night that I called the pediatrician to ask if something was wrong. They told me I was just lucky. During the day, I was lucky enough to have Sixto's help.

During those long, awful months of screaming colic, he would hold her tiny body on his forearm and walk around and around until she finally fell asleep.

I had severe second thoughts about what I'd gotten myself into. But he was still reassuring three months later when I went back to work—even though she was still screaming through most of every day.

I was lucky here, too. He gave up his job at the church so he could stay home and take care of her.

I went back to work at the newspaper, pumped milk in the restroom, and—though I would not have admitted it—was very, very happy to leave the fussy baby with her father.

He actually believed she'd stop crying one day.

He was right about that, too. His faith just seemed to work better than mine did.

So I always figured I'd leave the negotiations with the Old Man to him.

CHAPTER SIXTEEN

As parents, we were determined to do it all exactly right, which made it all so much harder.

We made our first trip to Mexico as would-be perfect parents when Lucy was a toddler. Doña Sole's house had been scrubbed and polished after the flood. She had a new, *mas o menos*, outhouse to replace the one that washed away, and one of her many granddaughters had bought her an upholstered couch and chair for the living room. Because the floor was still dirt, there was an adobe brick under each wooden leg of the couch and chair. That was to keep the termites from going up through the floor and eating the wood.

Four people sat hip-to-hip on the couch, and Sixto perched on one of the wide arms. On the other arm sat Trini, who was on one of his increasingly less frequent visits home from the United States. They were animated, and Sixto cued the laugh lines by touching Ana, who was on the couch next to him. A gentle tap on the knee. An open palm laid gently on the shoulder. He'd deliver his punch line and double up with laughter. These were familiar stories—family tales—about his father, his siblings, second cousins. Doña Sole was the first to explode into laughter—a lusty sound that must have filled the angels with impure envy. Nothing celestial could ever comprehend such a fleeting, earthy pleasure as my mother-in-law's laugh.

Doña Sole's American grandchild was sleeping behind the cloth curtain, but the noise was no problem. Once she checked out for the evening, Lucy was gone until dawn. Not even the laughter of a houseful of relatives could wake her.

At home, she had an oak crib that we had carefully researched to make sure the slats were not dangerously far apart and that the wood finish did not contain toxic residue. Here she slept on Doña Sole's single bed with pillows tucked in tightly on either side so she wouldn't roll. Just for good measure, Doña Sole had placed two of her dining room chairs with their ladder-backs against the edge of the bed and stacked our suitcases on the seats so the chairs would not move. This meant fewer seats for guests, but babies always came first in this house. Especially Sixto's baby.

The front and back doors were open wide, as they had been since the chilly dawn, when Doña Sole got up and started the day by sweeping the fallen mango and avocado leaves into a pile at the back of her house. It was too late in the year to worry about mosquitos, so Doña Sole's doors remained open after the sun disappeared and the single lightbulb hanging from the ceiling took over the job of illuminating our gathering. Family members and neighbors came and went, saying hello to me and my husband and peering past the curtain to exclaim "¡Que grande!" or "¡Que bonita!" after seeing our daughter. I sat at the table over a cup of tea. It wasn't hard to follow these stories. I'd heard them all before in English. I knew the punch lines.

This one was about a time when Sixto's younger siblings—Carlos, Ana, Emilia, and Luis—were all sick with measles. Sixto and Trini took turns describing how the younger ones were lined up side by side in one bed—probably the bed my daughter was in. They had fever and they ached. When one of them moved, the others cried out in protest. Ana and Emilia, who were there that evening, recalled the depth of their misery. Taking them to the doctor was never an option. It was too expensive and too impractical to transport four sick children into town by bus.

Instead, Toñita, who was a young adult then, took the bus into Mochis. At the hospital, they showed her how to give injections and sent her off with vials of medicine. As Toñita readied the syringe, Carlos bolted from the bed. They had to hold him down when they caught him. Toñita began wiping his haunch with alcohol in preparation for giving the injection. At the touch of the alcohol, Carlos began screaming.

"*¡Hasta mi hueso!*" Into my bone!

Sixto could barely get the words out. His mother was screaming with laughter at the memory of the way her son had yelled that the cotton ball felt like a needle going all the way into his bone. If the doors hadn't been open, Doña Sole's laughter would have sent them flying off the hinges. A shut-up house would not have been able to contain the laughter that night. As the uproar petered into chortles, Trini repeated: "*¡Hasta mi hueso!*" and the house shook with laughing again.

I loved watching them enjoy this story.

But, as usual, I was conflicted by First-World angst. Was it safe for a scarcely trained young woman to give injections to sick children? Should I feel the guilt of the privileged at hearing this story? And then there was the pathos of knowing what had happened to the little boy who'd run from the shot. Carlos had disappeared into the United States like so many others in search of a better life. No one had heard from him for years.

But that night, in Doña Sole's living room, Carlos was a child again. On another day—perhaps tomorrow—his mother and his siblings might lament and worry over where he was and whether he was well. But at this moment, there was only the fun of a happy memory gleaned out of a time of sickness and poverty.

Sixto was a master at coaxing joy out of pain. That was his gift, along with his great faith.

I knew he saw the lie in that laughter. And he didn't like to lie. He'd lived his new-world life long enough to understand the injustice in the old world he'd left behind. And he didn't like injustice, either.

That morning, Sixto and I had walked to the elementary school—it was the same one he and his siblings had attended, and it was still the only one in the ejido. It still lacked plumbing, just as it did when he was there. Children whose parents sometimes didn't have money for beans were still expected to bring pesos every day to pay for bottled water. The school was still white, but he said it used to look much better. The paint was old and chipping, and some of the windows grinned back at us with jagged edges.

We watched as the children marched in formation out front

with the Mexican flag. They walked in tight lines, holding their palms perpendicular to their hearts, singing about the glories of a country that did little to offer them much hope of a future. These patriotic young Mexicans would likely wind up washing dishes, butchering chickens, and busing tables in the United States.

Sixto said he was ashamed of the condition of the school.

When he was growing up, his father and the men in the village kept it painted and in good repair. There were no broken windows then. No trash in the corners. The outhouse was *mas o menos*.

But now the men were gone to el otro lado. Or maybe they—like their government—just didn't see much point in expending time and energy on poor kids. This school was a mute testament to the fact that Mexico was doing its best to get the poor to head north and send money back south.

I wrote about these things as a member of the editorial board of the *Arizona Daily Star* and then the *Arizona Republic*. Immigration was my beat. That was my job. But it was academic. It was about the promises of successive Mexican presidents to make education a priority. Reality was the look on Sixto's face as we walked around a school full of kids who deserved better.

My husband had attended this school when it had been simple, but cared for. Now my nieces and nephews were struggling to get ready for life in a school that looked like nobody cared at all.

I could see the shadow of that knowledge darken Sixto's face as he led his family through another happy story. But his joy was one of the reasons so many people came to visit Doña Sole's house when we were there. He never let them see his pain.

I was not surprised to see another visitor walking toward the open door.

But as this approaching stranger's silhouette filled the threshold, I could see that he had an assault rifle slung over his shoulder.

Sixto was still talking, but his words became meaningless gibberish to me. I wanted to run into the bedroom to throw myself over my sleeping child, but I was frozen in my chair. I wanted to scream and alert the others, but the sound cowered in my throat. I watched as this well-armed stranger surveyed a room full of in-laws and the man I loved.

Then my mother-in-law noticed him.

"¡Hijo!" she exclaimed with enthusiasm.

She motioned him over as she began clearing a space at the end of the dining room table. The guy took the gun off his shoulder and leaned it against the wall. By the time he sat down, Doña Sole was in the kitchen warming tortillas.

She brought him a big bowl of the cocido we'd enjoyed for dinner, along with some tortillas wrapped in a towel. Then she got him a cup of hot water with a spoon across the top. He hunched over the bowl, dipping the folded tortilla and eating without a word. Doña Sole jerked her head at the jar of instant coffee in front of me and I pushed it in his direction. Still chewing, he nodded at me and spooned the brown crystals into his cup.

Everyone else was quiet, but Doña Sole kept up a running conversation as she served him. I thought she was trying to keep him eating to delay the moment when he would gun us down. Maybe she figured he'd fall into a stupor and we could overpower him. She kept bringing him tortillas and refilling his bowl.

He was very young and without the gun over his shoulder, he looked like another nephew. As his eating slowed down, Sixto began to make conversation. My husband recognized from his accent that he was from somewhere to the south—a town far away—and they talked about that. The other details came out between spoonsful.

He'd been assigned to Los Suárez to help put up a big water tank in the field behind Doña Sole's house. He was staying with a family on the other side of the irrigation canal, but they fed him poorly. Someone recommended Doña Sole's good cooking. So now he paid her to give him good food in a quiet atmosphere. No houseful of kids. No sermons about finding Jesus. No political discussions. Just a great meal with a nice woman who regarded cooking as an art form and hospitality as a happy duty. He was one of several soldier/workers who had been coming here for the last few weeks.

Even though it was clear we were in no danger, I went to have a look at my daughter. She was sleeping in her pillow nest. Gracias a Dios.

The water tank that the soldier was helping to construct was a very big deal. Gravity would deliver running water to any of the villagers who could find pipe to hook up to it. This was a tangible reward from a grateful government to a community that had voted the right way in the last election. Because a new election would take place about the time the tank was finished, it was also a handy reminder of the benefits of supporting your friends in government. These cynical sentiments about Mexican politics were universal among the people we talked to. But nobody was complaining. Not really. They knew that when the tank was finished, life would improve enormously. No more hand-pumping water from questionable wells or carrying buckets from the pesticide-contaminated canal. Most people would still buy bottled water for drinking—nobody said the water the government would pump into the new tank would be that clean. But for everything else, a hose in the front yard would put flowing water at Doña Sole's command for the first time in her life. In the meantime, she made a little extra money by preparing food for the workers.

CHAPTER SEVENTEEN

A s our daughter grew up, we tried to make at least two trips a year to see Doña Sole.

Most of the trips involved family celebrations, which were planned long in advance to facilitate the schedules of those, like us, who were living in the United States. Almost everyone in Los Suárez had a family member or two working in the United States. In the 1990s, it was easy enough to go home to Mexico for the holidays—even those who did not have papers could sneak back across the border to their jobs with relatively little trouble.

So Christmas and Easter became popular times for weddings and *quinceañeras*.

It was December when Ana and Manuel's daughter had her fifteenth-birthday celebration. Lucy was still young enough to wear one of those frilly dresses with the crinoline slips that Artemia sent her every year as a way of showing her gratitude. Artemia and Porfirio's daughter Maria had come to stay with us for a year when Lucy was a toddler. Maria had wanted to study English so she could be more employable in Mexico. It worked. After her time with us, she returned to get a good job at a hotel that catered to Americans.

The first dress from Artemia came by mail the year Maria was with us. It was pale blue and white with lace and ruffles. It fit Lucy perfectly and she loved wearing it to go watch my mother square-dance. Lucy's skirt was as big as the ones on her grandmother's square-dance dresses. She loved that dress and wore it as often as I'd let her. Every year after that, Artemia would take

Lucy shopping in downtown Mochis, and they would find the fanciest dress with the biggest slip that any of us could imagine. She also bought matching hair bows. This lasted until Lucy outgrew the style at about seven or eight.

So Lucy was younger than that, and still outfitted in frills and a satin sash when we walked into the church for Mardi's quince. I'd learned how to produce a spit-and-polish family without plumbing. I was wearing a dark blue crepe dress with rhinestones on the bodice. Such embellishments were a no-guilt way around the no-jewelry rule. But I wore bracelets and earrings, anyway. Manuel was used to it; he didn't give them a second glance anymore. Sixto was wearing a new suit. We were appropriately elegant in the church.

Lucy sat in the aisle with one of Emilia's girls as her tío Manuel presided over the ceremony. It was a celebration of young womanhood—in the old days, an announcement that a girl was ready for marriage. These days, it was a fancy occasion to create the illusion that fifteen-year-olds are ready to put away childish things. Culturally speaking, it is a very big deal.

Manuel gave a nice talk. But he apparently had not entirely given up on me—his lack of interest in my jewelry notwithstanding. At one point, he deviated from his discussion about the proper role for a young woman in modern Mexico to give a discourse on parenting. He pointed out that some people—he looked at us—may limit themselves to one child because they think having a second would somehow diminish their love for the first. Manuel, the father of two, said he had learned that love expands to cover the second child. He didn't love his son any less after his daughter was born, he explained. What's more, each child was enriched by learning to share with the other. He went on at some length with his friendly reminder that God loves the fruitful. Manuel clearly thought I needed to get the Egyptian disease again.

I nudged Sixto, and we exchanged amused looks. It had become a running joke. Every time we returned to Mexico, we heard the same thing—¿Solo la única? Just the one? This didn't come from Doña Sole, Toñita, or the really close family, mind you. But from more distant interested parties. Or even those who should have been disinterested. That included waiters at the Santa Anita Hotel restaurant, where we went on every visit to have coffee and dessert and say hello to people Sixto used to work with. They'd greet me and Lucy, then look at Sixto and say: ¿Solo la unica? Sixto, who grew up with thirteen brothers and sisters, would say one was enough "for the experience."

After Manuel wrapped up the ceremony, several hundred people arrived at Doña Sole's for the party. This was a Mennonite quinceañera, so there was no dancing and no drinking. But there was plenty of eating, talking, and laughing.

The guests settled in under the mango trees at metal tables and chairs that had been rented and delivered for the occasion. I joined the kitchen crew to serve them; the actual preparation of the food had been going for days in advance. I might have liked an apron—I'd paid a bundle for this dress and I was hoping to use it again. But the other women who were getting ready to serve were also in their best, and nobody seemed worried about aprons. So I took my place at an enormous cauldron in the kitchen and began ladling barbacoa onto plastic plates. I handed each plate to Toñita, who spooned on some macaroni salad and a scoop of beans and passed it along for the addition of salsa fresca and tortillas. This all happened quicker than I can write about it. There were nieces and nephews waiting at the kitchen door to carry armloads of plates out to the waiting guests. Another crew of relatives was filling plastic cups with Coke—the brand name, not generic—and rushing out with beverages for the guests.

Emilia's daughters—Daniela, Tanya, and Anayetzi—and our Lucy flocked through the house from time to time, only to be shooed back outside with an admonition to sit somewhere and eat. Sixto was wandering from table to table, playing host and working the crowd with Manuel. He would rather talk to the tías than huddle behind the house with the tíos who were passing a bottle in a brown paper bag. As for Manuel, it was his duty as the daddy of the quinceañera to be a benevolent presence. Neither he nor Sixto drank anything stronger than that awful instant coffee.

As I handed Toñita what seemed like the thousandth plate, she told me I should add a little extra. The serving was done, she said, and this plate was for me. She added generous helpings of the rest of the meal as I straightened up and stretched my back. Then I followed her outside, where she found me a nice seat at a table that had just been vacated. I waited while she went inside for her own meal and a plate for Sixto, who had not taken time to sit down. The old people were drifting off, full, happy, and ready to tell anyone who wasn't there what a wonderful event they'd missed. The young people were pushing back the empty tables and making space for games. Toñita's oldest daughter, Maribel, directed them to set up two rows of chairs.

You all know how this game is played, she announced.

And they did. The light from the house spilled out to illuminate their enthusiastic game of musical chairs. I thought it odd to see teenagers so animated about a game I would plan for a five-year-old's party. But they embraced it with the same enthusiasm that they embraced the idea that when a tío or tía entered the room, they were supposed to jump up and give that person their chair.

Lucy came over to watch me eat, her eyes heavy. Emilia's three daughters surrounded her, wide awake and wondering what was next. They followed us into the house as I got my child ready for bed, peppering us with ¿Por que? at every stage of a rather mundane process of washing up, brushing teeth, changing into jammies. It was a question game that I didn't feel like playing. I told them all to be quiet or they'd have to leave before the bedtime story. Then they draped themselves silently around the bed and listened intently while I read an alphabet book about dinosaurs. Lucy was asleep before we got past "C" for Compsognathus. I quietly ushered Emilia's girls out, promising to finish the story later.

The guests were mostly gone now. Some of the women were cleaning up the kitchen. The men were folding up the tables and chairs and stacking them against the trees. Somebody—thankfully not Sixto—would sleep outside to keep an eye on them that night. The next morning, the rental company would send a truck to load them up and take them to the next party.

By midafternoon, things would be back to normal. Doña Sole would call across to Doña Mariyita that she had hot water in the kettle, and Doña Mariyita would walk over with an empty coffee cup and some cream or sugar to contribute to their daily get-together. Sixto asked his mother if this was the day that Doña Lencha—the most renowned baker in the ejido—was making pan dulce. She did a quick mental calculation that was designed to create suspense. Then Sixto ran off to get us all some fine sweet bread to go with the instant coffee.

It all seemed timeless. But time did pass.

Lucy was in kindergarten when Maria announced she was getting married. She was eager for us to meet the young man when we came to visit at New Year's. He was tall, polite, and they were very, very much in love. He had a good job with the national railroad, so they had prospects of continuing the climb into the middle class that Porfirio had begun with his move into the city. Maria and Diego were planning an August wedding, and they wanted Lucy to be flower girl.

We had to say no, because attending the Sunday wedding would mean Lucy could not possibly be home in time for the first day of first grade, which was Monday. Sixto and I thought school should be the priority. Boring, unimaginative parents, we were still obsessed with doing everything right. As the months passed, I regretted the decision. What would Lucy remember longer? The first day of a long school year? Or the wedding of the cousin who had taught her to sing "El Oso Subio la Montaña"? We went with the oso.

On the day of the wedding, we arrived at Porfirio's house early so that Lucy could try on the dress Toñita made, using only the measurements Sixto had given her over the phone. I didn't expect it to fit; I made a lot of Lucy's clothes in those days, but I used a pattern and we always had numerous fittings to make sure everything was right. Toñita, as usual, was a model of how things should be done. The dress she made for Lucy was a perfect fit—although I did notice with some perverse satisfaction that the zipper was not quite as finished at the neck as I would have made it.

We hung the dress back up—along with my long purple formal and Sixto's latest new suit—next to the other wedding finery in the closet that Maria and her sisters must have emptied for the occasion.

There was a long day of preparations ahead.

The room Maria shared with her three sisters was both a haven from the hubbub of houseguests and an anthill of its own activity. There was a lot going on in that room. At a table against the wall, the pastry chef was frosting the layers of the wedding cake. Her hand mixer whirred and stopped, whirred and stopped as she whipped up the royal icing and put together components of what would later be assembled into an elaborate, sprawling display with bridges, columns, and pathways. A hairstylist was also set up in that bedroom to do bridesmaids' hair. She had a chair next to the bed, with her blowers, curlers, combs, brushes, and travel cases of hairpins and products all around her. One by one, the members of the wedding party were adorned with towering mounds of hair that swirled and curled in remarkable ways not seen in nature.

Maria fussed about her French twist, making several trips to the living room to tell her mother the tiara for the veil wasn't going to sit right. Each time I could hear Sixto's voice, and then the room full of people would erupt into laughter. Maria would come back to us, still insisting something was wrong and begging for ideas on how to improve her hair. She didn't believe me when I said it looked great.

I also thought Lucy's hair was just fine, too. But the consensus in that room was that this little girl needed much more than the few curls I'd added with a curling iron that morning. She took her seat in the styling chair, and after a great deal of teasing, twisting, spraying, and pinning, she had a rising mass of curls so elaborate I wasn't sure her white straw hat would fit anymore. But it did.

The room was a mixture of smells, any one of which would have been powerful on its own. Together, they went perfectly with the dizzying array of activities. The cake and sugar frosting was one layer of aroma. The hairspray and nail polish was another. Over it all were exotic scents from pretty bottles. Maria had saved up to buy Estee Lauder "Beautiful" perfume. The smell got lost in the cloud of scents, so she kept spraying more. When the door of the bedroom opened, the smell of chili and beans and tortillas floated in. Artemia had been cooking for her houseguests since before dawn.

A little boy in a miniature black tuxedo would periodically open the door and bring us those cooking smells. He'd smile for the girls as they pinched his cheeks and told him he was *muy guapo*. Then he'd wait for them to get distracted so he could dip his fingers into the frosting bowl. Once discovered, he was ejected. But he came back several times with his innocent look fully intact. The woman assembling the cake was remarkably good-natured about this violation of her creative space until he began running his finger along the frosted edge of the cake. Then his mother was summoned from the party in the living room to make sure he did not return.

I wasn't part of the wedding party, and I didn't have so many preparations to make. But I stayed in that little room for a couple of very good reasons. First, Lucy wanted me there, and I knew the girls very well and I enjoyed their lively company. Second— and perhaps most important—the little room had a cooler in the window. It was a sweltering August day in the rest of the house.

When it came time to change into their finery, each bridesmaid hid behind the closet door to put on her dress. The modesty seemed silly—we were all female after the little boy had been permanently banished. But the modesty was contagious. When it was my turn to change, I hid myself and so did Lucy.

Artemia took a break from serving the houseguests to help Maria get into her dress. This was a major endeavor, and Maria could not hide. She had to stand on the bed to step into her massive hoop slip and arrange the cloud of a wedding dress so that the train could be carefully held above the floor until it was time to walk down the aisle. She looked beautiful. But there wasn't much time to think about it then.

Rows of cars were waiting to drive us to the church.

When we got to the church, however, we had plenty of time to think.

The groom waited alone on the altar for a full hour before Porfirio and Maria made their entrance. Like the rest of us, he had to be roasting in those fancy clothes—there was no evaporative cooler, let alone air-conditioning. But he maintained his decorum. He waited with a good-natured patience. Knowing Maria as I did, I thought maybe she was training her groom for a lifetime of waiting. She's a lovely and charming young woman, but she was rarely ready on time during the year she spent with us.

I was wrong, though.

The holdup was Porfirio.

After a day of sharing congratulatory toasts back behind the truck—Artemia would never permit drinking in the house—Maria's father was feeling particularly emotional. He was overcome at the sight of his daughter in her wedding gown, and suddenly stricken with that parental sense of having done too little in those few years when parents are called on to do so much. He'd been a good father, and Maria tried to console him in the little "bride's room" off the narthex. But he resisted consolation. After awhile, someone came to get Artemia, who was seated in the front row, two pews in front of us. She walked quickly to the back of the church, and returned a few minutes later without responding to any of those who tried to catch her attention with whispered hisses.

We waited some more.

When the music finally started, all eyes turned to the back of the church. There, in the doorway, stood my little girl with a basket of flowers. It was her first major performance before a big audience. She stood there for what seemed like a very long time, and I got really nervous. She's frozen in fear, I thought. What should I do? I was ready to go into full panic mode, but Sixto remained calm. Unlike me, he took the time to notice that she looked serene as she bided her time.

Then, on just the right beat, she began slowly walking down the aisle, dropping flowers and petals. She did it smoothly, and with great drama. My camera was in my hand, but I just stood there with my mouth open. I was overcome. Like Porfirio.

Lucy took her place at the front of the church and the music began again. The little boy in the tuxedo led the procession of bridesmaids and their escorts. Again, it was so painfully slow you'd never have suspected we'd been waiting an hour. I'd sort of lost track of the real purpose of the gathering, if you know what I mean. By now, I was ready to get this over with so I could go and change into comfortable shoes.

Then Maria and Porfirio appeared and I snapped back into the moment. He was composed, but still red-faced. It didn't matter. She was glowing with new hope even from behind the veil. It's that naked hope—and the knowledge of how far it is from real life—that makes people cry at weddings. The one tissue I'd gotten out after Lucy's walk was already damp, so I fished out another Kleenex from my purse.

Like most church services, it went on too long, though.

After the ceremony, Toñita insisted we rush over to the rented hall where the reception was being held so we'd get a good seat. Lucy missed the reenactment of the wedding and the photo shoot in the plaza because of that—and we waited at the hall for at least another hour until the wedding party arrived. Toñita need not have worried. There was plenty of seating for the several hundred guests, and plenty of food. I don't know if Artemia had a hand in preparing everything that came out of that kitchen, but she certainly played a role in supervising the serving.

That night, when I took the hairpins out of Lucy's hair, we counted more than sixty of them. What's more, her hair was so well sprayed that it stayed in place even without the pins.

CHAPTER EIGHTEEN

After that, the years were like bridesmaids before the wedding—rushing with a manic focus on some future event. Some deadline. Some goal that was wrapped up in bigger dreams and breathless hopes—hopes that didn't always have a foothold in facts or experience.

Sixto earned his bachelor's in education and started teaching elementary school. He became such a good teacher that parents would petition his principal to let him move up to the next grade and teach their children another year. He did this several times.

When a group of students he'd had for three years was ready to move on, the parents arranged a school's-out party at the park. They brought tables full of homemade food and hired a little train to take the kids on rides around the grassy hills.

Sixto introduced me, and the parents would gush about what a wonderful teacher he was. Many pulled me aside while he busy setting up the piñata to tell me again how much it had meant for their child to have my husband as a teacher. They loved him.

He taught in low-income areas where a lot of the families spoke only Spanish. But his expectations for these kids were sky-high. He was troubled because he saw many Spanish-dominant children classified as learning disabled.

"They are smart kids, mi amor," he would tell me. "They just don't understand English."

He began a master's in bilingual learning disabilities because he wanted to gain enough expertise to help make sure the kids who got put in special education really needed to be there. In one school, he initiated a system for evaluating children before they got labeled as learning disabled. He called it a "pre-referral intervention program." The goal was to identify children whose challenge was solely related to language deficiencies, and get them some help with English instead of just referring them to special education programs.

On Saturdays, Lucy and I would spend the days together so he could study in peace. She did all the normal extracurricular stuff: gymnastics, soccer, diving, art classes, horseback riding—and endless birthday parties for school friends and neighbor children. Her own birthday parties were a study in excess. For several, Sixto insisted we hire a stretch limo to transport little girls from the miniature golf course to our house.

On Sundays, we went to church. At least for a while we did. Little by little, Sixto began to lose interest in church. Lucy went to the Catholic Church with her grandmother.

My mother's desert acre had appreciated over the years as the city grew closer to her. The area had changed, too. Her like-minded, friendly neighbors were dying off or selling out. The new people were more secretive and less social—more like survivalists than the independent, desert-loving folks who initially moved out there. My mother sold her place and bought a little house in town—seven houses down from our house. She immediately began spreading wildflower seeds in the backyard.

Lucy and my mother were best pals. Our daughter spent as many hours with Grandma as possible.

My mother picked her up after school, and the two of them made excursions to the zoo or the park when the weather was cool enough. In the spring and fall, when it was too hot, they devised all sorts of games at Grandma's house, including playing blackjack for chips—something my mother said would help Lucy learn math. When I finished my work for the day, I'd walk down the hill to get her. I'd usually have a cup of tea or a beer with my mother while we waited for Sixto to stop by on his way home. When he had night class at the university, my mother would sometimes cook dinner for the three of us.

These were busy, predictable days.

We had lavish holiday dinners at my mother's house for Easter and Thanksgiving, and Christmas at our house. When we went to Mexico, Sixto, Lucy, and I walked into a big, collective hug from people whose exact relationships to my husband I sometimes still had trouble remembering. (Okay, so tell me again: she's your sister's husband's cousin's daughter, but she calls me Tía even though you are really not her uncle.)

Every year, Gavino would slaughter a pig that had been eating table scraps for months in a comfortable wallow in Toñita's back yard. We'd have a feast to remember, then I'd convince everyone to line up for another group photograph.

Every trip, we'd bring a gift from my mother to Doña Sole and take back Doña Sole's gift to La Señora. Most of the time, both ladies would stash away the gift for safekeeping.

These events marked the years with loving bookmarks. Routines get a bad reputation, and I have to admit that I sometimes longed for a break from the same old, same old. But there is an opiate in sameness. You forget time will catch up with you.

I didn't see the little changes that were leading up to a massive stroke, which, like the last chime of a clock at midnight, left an awful silence behind. I thought my mother would always be there to share a cup of tea or make pork chops in mushroom sauce for Lucy and me on Monday nights when Sixto was in class at the university.

My mother died two months before Lucy turned ten. Sunday, March 18, 2001.

I didn't know it until Monday, though.

I'd spent the day in my home office writing an editorial that was designed to convince the legislature not to cut services for children—a relatively futile effort in a conservative state where Republican lawmakers thought it was their solemn duty to starve the beast of government. Futility was my specialty. I wrote about child welfare, domestic violence, early childhood education, juvenile delinquency—and immigration, of course. Arizona's political "leaders" were usually on the mean side of all those issues.

Nature was always on my side, though. The days were getting longer as the wildflowers began to emerge. It was still light as I shut my laptop and called it a day.

"Today, I need a cup of chamomile tea," I told Amber, our

little beagle-Jack Russell mix, as I hooked up her leash for the short walk down to get Lucy.

I was hoping for an invitation to dinner. The day had left me drained and tired for no particular reason. I was looking forward to the jolt of energy my mother and my daughter delivered when they were together. It was never dull when the two of them were hatching something, and they were always hatching something.

The dog pulled at her leash until we got to the sidewalk in front of the house. Then she stopped and looked back at me.

Even from there, we could tell something was wrong. The front drapes were shut. My mother always kept them open in the daytime, and there was still plenty of light. She had told me more than once that a darkened house reminded her of the wake after her mother died. She would not have shut the drapes this early.

Amber and I walked through the carport, past her truck and into the backyard.

It looked wrong, too. The drape across the sliding glass patio door was pulled shut. My mother's black Belgian Sheepdog pushed it aside and stood barking at my little dog and me from inside.

Kelly never barked at us.

I didn't see any sign of my mother or Lucy, but they had to be in there. It was way past time to pick up Lucy, and the truck was in the carport. If they'd gone for a walk, they would have taken Kelly. I had a key, but I knocked, anyway. Kelly went ballistic, jumping and pawing the glass door. I was afraid she'd break it, so I used my key and unlocked the door. The dog nearly knocked me over running out. She dashed to a patch of grass and squatted. She apparently had been waiting to pee for a very long time.

I began to get scared.

I called out to my mother and Lucy. I could hear the television. It was turned up way too high, and it wasn't tuned to one of the PBS kids' shows Lucy loved.

Amber had run in the house as Kelly ran out. She came back out now, with an odd and frightened posture. I held the curtain back and looked in. The living room lights were on.

I called again. The dogs were both next to me now, one on each side. They looked up at me, like dogs do, waiting for a cue.

I didn't want to go in. So I called again. But I knew nobody was going to answer.

It's not a big house, but it took me a long time to cross the living room. I stopped to turn off the TV; it was too loud. Some damn afternoon talk show that my mother never would have watched. I went to the corner to turn off the lamp. She never used lights in the daytime.

Then I made myself go around the corner.

She was lying in the hall. Her beautiful green eyes were wide open and seeing nothing.

"Oh, my God. Oh, my God," I kept saying to the dogs, who watched me from across the room. They didn't come close. They'd already seen the truth. Smelled the death.

The woman who answered my 911 call made me touch my mother to be sure she was dead. But it really wasn't necessary. She'd been dead since the night before.

But where was my daughter?

I tried to call the school, but it was past the hour when they closed the after-care room and began charging a dollar per minute for kids not picked up. Nobody answered. As I hung up the phone, it rang. It was Lucy's teacher.

"Is something wrong?" she said. They had been calling for hours, she said. Lucy had told her not to call me at home because I was working. How silly, I thought. How like an overdramatic preteen.

The teacher listened silently as I whispered what happened. I was still waiting for the police, I said, but I'd come for Lucy as soon as they left.

"I'll bring her home," the teacher told me. I could see her in my mind's eye, with her long red hair, her cargo pants, and her almost too-sincere manner. Teaching was a sacred mission for her, like it was for Sixto.

"Tell her I'm at her grandmother's house. Bring her there," I said. Then I added: "Don't tell her."

The police were official and professional. It was easy to see what happened. An old lady died while getting ready for bed. They promised to send a van around to pick up the body, and warned me not to look for a nice, shiny ambulance. They didn't send the good vehicles for dead people, apparently.

The teacher's car pulled up.

I don't want my daughter in this house with her dead grand-mother, I told the cops.

Go ahead, they said, you can come back to lock up when you see the van pull up.

"How do I tell her that her favorite person in the world is dead?" I said.

I was in that unnaturally calm place where you go first when unspeakable tragedy hits. That place of unexplainable clarity. My mind was methodically taking me through the motions, making sure I did the things that needed to be done. My emotions were circling like wild things, waiting their chance to rush in and de-vour me. But not yet. In this instant, a kind of numbness allowed me to function. I had to get my daughter home. I had to get this done. Sixto was in some classroom at the university, and neither of us had cell phones. There was just me and the dogs to guide my little girl and me through the greatest tragedy either of us had ever faced. My mother was dead; I had to be the mother.

The cop spoke in that matter-of-fact tone that cops use to try to keep people in that numb and controlled mental state.

"Sometimes it's best to just say it without trying to hide any-thing," one of them said.

I rushed out the door as Lucy was getting out of the car.

"What's wrong?" she said.

"Let's go home," I said. And I took her hand as we began walking up the hill.

"Where's Grandma? What's wrong?"

I thought of the cop's advice.

"Grandma's dead," I said.

At that moment, I could see the whole scene as though I were standing next to the teacher at the bottom of the hill. As though I were the cop looking at us from the front door of my mother's house. Or maybe it was as though my mother were watching from her front yard.

I saw a woman and her daughter hand in hand, walking slow-ly, talking. There was a beagle on a leash on one side and a black dog with a flowing tail on the other. Their heads were down, even the dogs'. The woman's head was inclined toward the child. Then the little girl's body slumped just a little, as though a heavy weight had been thrown across her shoulders. They stopped and looked at each other. The woman shook her head. I'm sorry. Then they kept on walking.

Lucy's music teacher played violin at the memorial service—Irish music, some happy and some sad, like life. Sixto broke down and wept several times when he went to the front of the church to talk about my mother. My sister and Devon came down, but when my sister found out my mother left her house to me, the growing estrangement between her and me reached a crescendo. She left and I never saw her again, although Devon came back into our lives years later, after my sister died.

None of us were ever the same after my mother died. But we pretended to be. Tried to be.

Lucy remained the polite and perfect child, balancing between two cultures, careful not to betray either one. She never confided in me the way I always confided in my mother, but I could see her heart ache for her grandmother.

I sought my solace in work.

I launched a campaign of home improvements.

We had the original 1950s kitchen in our house redone. We tiled the living room. I painted the walls over and over until I got them the right color. I sewed curtains, bought rugs, reupholstered furniture.

This was an opiate of activity designed to kill the pain.

After awhile, I realized I was making all these changes so my mother would be impressed the next time she dropped by. My head knew that was never going to happen. It took years for my heart to believe it.

Even now, when I hang a new picture on the wall, I can imagine how she'd exclaim about how great it looks—as though nobody else in the world could have picked out such a great picture and found such a perfect place for it. Perfect. She always thought I was perfect.

Her absence was a crater in my soul. I looked to Sixto to fix it. His hotline to heaven had served me well all these years. But his faith wasn't as bright and shining as it used to be.

He missed her, too.

Sixto loved my mother. In many ways, she was more of an anchor for him in the new world than I was. She was steadier, more predictable. She served him Coke and ice cream without the lecture about sugar and calories. She dropped everything when we came to visit. Unlike me, she never let on that she might have something better to do—even when she did.

Her death hit Sixto hard. The unfairness of it. The suddenness.

CHAPTER NINETEEN

There was no noise from the kitchen, and Doña Sole's coughing had stopped.

There was just the sound of Sixto and Lucy breathing, unsynchronized and untroubled.

How much of that had been a dream? Was there a monster in the corner?

Worse yet, what would it mean if the monster were gone from this now-silent house?

I opened my eyes in the dark room.

I pushed myself up slowly to take a look.

It was almost a relief to see him still there. That hideous, misshapen face still waited in the corner. Eyes shut. Mouth unable to speak. Had he at least heard my story? Could he even hear?

You bastard, I thought. You sweep in and take my mother and dare to come back now? I've known you since I was twenty years old. You are dumb and clumsy. You take the wrong people at the wrong time. And you don't care.

"You will leave here with nothing but the chicken," I hissed. "Nothing but the chicken."

Sixto's sleep breathing paused, and I realized I'd spoken out loud. I put my head back down and waited for him to slip back into his sleep rhythm.

Then I would tell Pancho Villa a thing or two.

This time, I wasn't afraid.

But I must have fallen asleep then, too, flush with my plan to tell off the vision in the corner.

The next thing I knew, Doña Sole was standing next to the bed, urging me to get up.

The night was finally over.

I looked at the corner. There was nothing in the gray but some dusty curtain rods. He was gone and we were all still here. I waited him out.

Doña Sole had put a cup of hot water for instant coffee on the table for me, along with fried eggs, beans, and fresh tortillas. The others had already finished by the time I sat down to eat. Sixto was loading the car. Lucy was putting her jammies in her suitcase. Doña Sole gave no sign of the rough night she'd had. She was happily wrapping up bean burritos for us to eat on the road.

When she said: "*¿Como amaneciste?*" I knew exactly what to say: "*Muy bien, muy cómodo.*" Very comfortable.

She assured me that she'd slept well, too. Gracias a Dios.

When I took my empty plate and cup to the kitchen, and looked around for the chicken, I half expected to see it dead under the crate. That was the deal, after all.

The green crate was turned open end up near the back door.

Where's the chicken? I asked.

Doña Sole shrugged.

She turned it loose, she said. She didn't feel like making caldo today.

PART TWO:
Life after Death

CHAPTER TWENTY

Doña Sole died slowly of cancer of the esophagus over the next ten months.

The coughing was a sign, but it was misread the first time she went to the doctor. Not long after we got home from tiling Doña Sole's bathroom, we were told she was going to have gallladder surgery. We were relieved that a fixable problem had been found and diagnosed, though I didn't see the connection between the gallbladder and coughing.

Nevertheless, she had the surgery and began a convalescence that Toñita carefully monitored.

She didn't get better, though.

Then came the news that the doctor had found cancer.

There was another operation and they took out part of her esophagus. She started her recovery at home, but that didn't work out. So she went to stay with Toñita to heal.

But she didn't heal.

No food stayed with her, though they tried all sorts of things. She began to slowly starve to death. Sixto made trips to Cohui bampo every few weeks—twelve long hours on the bus Friday night and twelve hours back to arrive late Sunday so he could be back in front of the classroom early Monday morning.

He never complained.

Before each trip, he'd look for some new kind of liquid nutrition drink, some new stomach acid pills. He'd pack them up with the hope that he'd found something that would help Doña Sole eat. He'd come back beaten down and bone weary. It wasn't just his mother who looked to him for strength. They were all leaning on him. All needy. Just like me.

We all went to see her at Christmastime, making a great pretense at normalcy.

There was the usual family gathering—but at Toñita's this time. They even invited the doctor who had operated on Doña Sole, treating him like a hero for having saved her.

They brought Doña Sole outside briefly. She looked tiny in a plush pink sweat suit that we'd brought for her. She was very still as she watched the gathering from a chair set against the house.

"*Pura familia*," she said, looking at all those people. They were the fruit of her life with a man who was waiting for her somewhere on the other side.

Sixto's brother Rosario was there with his second wife and their son, but he was not the same man whose happiness shone so brightly the day he and Luz Maria took us to the beach. Their marriage ended with great bitterness, and he seemed uncomfortable to be so close to the house where Luz Maria still lived.

Toñita had severed all ties with Luz Maria after the divorce and erected a barrier of anger that none of her family dared openly cross—even Gavino, who was Luz Maria's brother. Sixto had brought them back together by gently reminding Toñita that she was not meant to be the judge of anybody. The relationship between Toñita and Luz Maria was never quite as cordial as it had been, but Gavino had his sister back.

From that point on, Gavino called Sixto *nuestro angel*—our angel.

Now they looked to their angel for a miracle.

The day after the party, Doña Sole gave us each her blessing, one by one, as she lay propped against the bed pillows.

This was her goodbye, and it was as gracious as her hellos had always been.

When she was done, Lucy remained sitting on the bed. She smiled at her sole remaining grandmother, pretending nothing was wrong. This was exactly what Doña Sole wanted her to do, and Lucy did it with remarkable grace and dignity. Lucy held her grandmother's hand.

Emilia's daughter Daniela stood at the end of the bed, weeping with great volume.

"*No llores*," Doña Sole said to her, with obvious annoyance.

Emilia had just loudly burst into tears and run out of the room. Doña Sole made it clear she did not appreciate the drama.

If Death behaved as a gentleman, he would have taken her then—after she gave her blessing, after she saw her large family gathered one last time.

But Doña Sole continued a painful and slow decline weeks after she said her goodbyes. There was at least one midnight rush to the hospital. But Doña Sole refused to stay there with tubes to keep her alive and strangers to poke at her. She made them take her back to Toñita's.

Sixto took a leave of absence so he could help Toñita nurse her back to health. They still believed that was possible, even after she grew too weak to drink.

This is where faith became a problem.

Sixto believed that believing was enough to overcome any-thing—especially when it came to his mother.

Shortly after we were married, he had told me a story about when he was a young man and his mother had a terrible tooth-ache. In that time and place, there were no dentists and there was no option to do anything but what they did. They prayed. He told her that he trusted in her strength. He read her the Bible through a long horrible night. Eventually, the terrible pain subsided. He chalked it up to prayer and faith. I knew from the years when I'd worked in a dentist's office that an abscessed tooth can stop hurt-ing after the infection destroys all the nerves in the tooth. Once the tooth is dead, it no longer feels any pain. I saw a rational explanation. He saw a miracle.

And he wanted another one.

This must have been when Sixto spent the last of his stockpile of faith.

He never accepted the horrible truth that no amount of prayer was going to change things. Maybe that's why Doña Sole took so long to die—maybe Death was being more of gentleman than I gave him credit for. Doña Sole was waiting for her children to say their goodbyes and mean it.

But she couldn't wait forever. She died in Sixto's arms.

This was the Miracle that Didn't Come. And it broke my husband's heart. Now was the time to lean on my faith, as we'd leaned on his all those years. No, it wasn't as bright and shining as his. It didn't sing out in beautiful tones that brought tears to people's eyes in church. Sometimes it hid behind layers of resentment. But it was sturdy. It was enduring. But he didn't lean on it. Instead, he held onto his disappointment over the failure of one more miracle to materialize on behalf of his mother.

When Sixto called to tell me she was gone, he could not get the words out.

I immediately began preparations for Lucy and me to join him. I called the kennel and reserved a spot for Kelly and Amber. I made arrangements to take time off work. I checked the buses.

Then Sixto called back and said: "Don't come." He said it would be too dangerous for us to travel alone.

We'll be okay, I insisted.

"Please, mi amor," he said. "I'll be crazy if I have to think of you and Lucy riding that bus by yourselves."

"We can fly," I said.

Don't come, he said again.

Toñita agreed it would be too dangerous. That became the final word. Toñita was the matriarch now.

Despite all that Doña Sole had done to make me feel like part of the family, I became the outsider that day. The interloper. The gringa who was thought incompetent to ride a bus with her daughter through Mexico.

So we waited, Lucy and I, until Sixto got back.

And resentment steeped inside me, along with the still-unresolved grief over my own mother's death.

When we picked him up from the bus station, Sixto carried pain that he thought he could not put down without insulting his mother. He immediately began talking about their plans—his and his siblings' plans for an ongoing tribute to their mother. They wanted to turn her house into a shrine where no one would live, but any family member could stay during visits. I was not part of the planning, but I was expected to embrace the idea—along with the implied responsibility that Sixto and I, as the most well-to-do of the family, would handle ongoing maintenance.

I hated this idea. It had been a labor of love to fix up a house where Doña Sole could live. I had no interest in continuing to fix it up as a monument. What's more, I thought Sixto—of all people—should understand this.

I had sold my mother's at a loss almost immediately after she died. I never wanted to walk through the door again. Not with my mother gone. Not without her at the kitchen sink, filling the kettle with water for tea and telling me to get the cookies out from the shelf under the microwave. At the time, Sixto said he understood completely.

He should have known I didn't want to see Doña Sole's house again, either. Not with her gone.

But here was this idea—fully formed and presented to me as we drove back from the bus station. I was cold to Sixto and his idea. I was angry at how easily he had excluded me from Doña Sole's funeral. I was bitter, too.

I hadn't finished mourning my own mother. Now our lives were being defined by Sixto's grief for his.

Death was taking over our lives.

Sixto and his siblings came up with a plan for Mother's Day that also left me feeling like the outsider. It rubbed me the wrong way for other reasons, as well. We drove to Toñita's with the sole purpose of honoring their dead mother. As Sixto's live wife and the mother of his child, I thought this was going a bit too far. Where was my celebration? Wasn't I a mother, too?

The drive down was grim.

As we got out of the car at Toñita's house, she embraced me tearfully.

"*Estamos solos*," she said. We are alone.

No, I thought, we are not. It's a sin to say we are.

But I did not dare to say it out loud. I was afraid Sixto agreed with her.

Toñita's grief was so heavy she could barely move. Toñita and Sixto went over those last months of Doña Sole's life, searching for the mistake they'd made, the cure they could have found, the negligence of which they must be guilty. They were sure they'd done something wrong. She hadn't been meant to die.

All those years of reading the Bible and singing at the church should have created a savings account of faith from which they could draw comfort and acceptance. But they'd spent it all on the hope that she would survive.

I came out swinging against grief, desperately trying to bury it in activity. But Sixto and his sister were inviting their grief to pull up a chair and stay for dinner.

I became even more the outsider as I watched them nourish each other's pain. I didn't dare talk about moving on. They were measuring the quality of their love for their mother by the depth of their mourning. They would judge me harshly if I said to them—as Doña Sole had said to Daniela—*no llores.*

I kept my mouth shut. And I felt guilty about my anger at them. I'd loved Doña Sole, too.

On Mother's Day morning, we drove to Doña Sole's house to water the roses and talk about all the repairs that were needed. They were determined to hold her spirit captive in that place so they could stand in the open front door and pretend she was just out back, hanging up clothes. They thought it was a good way to honor her. I thought it was a horribly inappropriate way to re-member a woman whose laughter was enough to crack the glass floor of heaven.

It was not my place to say that. So I didn't.

But even thinking it opened a space between Sixto and me that never before existed.

By the time we left to drive back to Tucson, even the obligatory stop at the fosa seemed like a cheerful interlude from the unre-mitting grief.

After we got home, Toñita called regularly. Each time it was the same. Sixto would tell her he'd call right back—so that we, not she, would pay the international call charge. Then they'd talk for a long time. After he hung up, he'd go to the Safeway to wire Toñita some money so she could take a *corona* of flowers to the cemetery.

Grief was not only sitting at the dinner table. It had unpacked its bags and moved in for good.

I tried to talk to him about it.

"I'm fine, mi amor," he'd tell me. But he wasn't.

One day he said he'd lost his faith.

I wanted to go back and find it. Pick it up and carry it home to him. Sprinkle it in his coffee. Dust it over his sleeping head to keep the pain away. I tried reading the Bible to him. He listened, but it didn't help.

This was the son Doña Sole named after the love of her life. She always said she had no favorites among her children, but anyone could see that Sixto was extra special to her. He was the one who could find any verse in scripture from a half quote. The one who had written out the entire New Testament on yellow pads just so he could take the time to think about the words. The Word. His mother's death had left it a closed book for him.

I needed to do something. I wasn't ready to let Pancho Villa win. He could have the dead. I wanted to reclaim the living.

CHAPTER TWENTY-ONE

I found a solution in an event that was as deeply embedded in the Mexican culture as the grief that was devouring my husband and his sister. I presented it as a way to honor his daughter and help his sister.

This was a powerful card and I played it masterfully. I manufactured this miracle.

Our daughter was going to turn fifteen that spring. We'd discussed and dismissed the idea of having a quinceañera for her in Tucson. Who would come? Some friends. Sure. My sister no longer spoke to me. Few of Lucy's Mexican relatives would be able to make the trip, and fewer still would have been able to get visas to make the trip legally.

What if we did it in Mexico?

This was my idea.

I presented it to Sixto this way: What if we gave Toñita a distraction for her grief, and asked her to do the planning and host the event at her house?

For the first time in a long time, Sixto didn't respond with an exasperated: "Oh, mi amor" or "No, mi amor."

He thought it was a good idea. So we asked Lucy.

Our daughter, the buoyancy of her adolescence clashing almost daily with the weight of my menopause, chewed over this parental offering and found nothing to dislike about the idea. In fact, she loved it.

So did Toñita.

Now her phone calls included more than the usual discussion

of her most recent trip to the cemetery and an assessment of how poorly the roses at Doña Sole's house were doing.

Now she and Sixto also talked about plans for a celebration. Now when Sixto hung up the phone, we discussed Toñita's ideas for how to arrange a quinceañera that Cohuibampo would long remember. We set the date for just after school let out in June of 2006. The guest list included three hundred-plus family and friends. You always had to include a "plus," Sixto said, because people brought friends and third cousins you might have forgotten.

The quniceñeara took over our lives with the breathless excitement of a teenage girl.

Sixto and Lucy made several trips to Cohuibampo to plan with Toñita. They had to reserve the church, arrange to rent the tables that would fill Toñita's front yard, hire a suitably respectable Mennonite band, and assure that the cousins who would serve dinner understood the gravity of their task and the importance of showing up in black pants, white shirts, and ties.

They talked to Toñita's daughter, Maribel, about presiding over the ceremony. This was my idea. Maribel was a preacher, and having her do the service instead of a male minister appealed to me on a variety of levels. I was thrilled she agreed so easily.

They talked to a pastry chef about the cake. They talked to a friend who had a special chair for the quinceañera that would be set up at the center of a long table where Lucy would be flanked by her fifteen *damas*. They reserved the time with the lady who would come to the house to do the girls' hair.

Ana volunteered to make table decorations—each table would have a pink candle in a glass holder surrounded by baby's breath and ribbon. She also bought hundreds of little plastic high-heeled shoes—some white, some pink, some crystal clear—and decorated them with ribbons and rosebuds. These would be collected by guests to remember the day our daughter gave away her childhood.

Gavino said he and his friends would handle the food. The pig they had been fattening up snuffled happily under a tree when we arrived, oblivious to the planning that was consuming the rest of us. I had no doubt the food would be amazing. Sixto was the angel, but Gavino called Lucy *la Reina*.

Life was winning. Then death played a high card.

Suddenly and unexpectedly, the granddaughter of Sixto's old-est sister died. She was young. She had come as a child with her mother to visit us one Christmas when Lucy was an infant. We took her and her mother to Winterhaven, a green-grass neighbor-hood in Tucson where all the families go overboard with lights and holiday decorations. In one front yard, a man was dressed as Santa to greet the children. My heart swelled when he approached this little girl from Mexico with a hearty "Feliz Navidad." How wonderful, I thought, for her to visit the United States and find a Spanish-speaking Santa.

Now that little girl, who'd been pursuing a career in college, was dead. Sixto said we'd have to cancel the quince. It would be too disrespectful to go on with a family celebration in the face of such a family tragedy.

We saw no other option.

However, as Lucy's stoic disappointment seeped into every fi-ber of the house, Sixto came up with an idea. First, he said, he'd have to run it by Toñita. When she agreed, he asked Lucy if she'd be willing to make one more trip by bus. They would go to visit the mother of the girl who died, and ask her permission to have the quinceañera.

This was the same granddaughter—Isabel—who bought Doña Sole the couch where Sixto and his siblings sat to tell stories about Carlos and the injection. She would have been entirely within her rights to enforce a moratorium on celebrations after her daugh-ter's death.

But she didn't. She told Lucy to have a good quinceañera, and then asked her to try to understand why she wouldn't be there to help enjoy the party.

It was a gracious blessing.

When Sixto and Lucy got back, we started shopping for her dress. She picked out pale pink, with pearl trim and a long, full skirt. The slip would have made Scarlett O'Hara envious. There were satin shoes, satin pillows, and a rhinestone tiara to go with it.

A quinceañera is like a wedding, except you get to take your daughter home when it's all over.

I resisted the matronly mother-of-the bride outfits Sixto thought were so appropriate. I left him at home and I picked out a long, form-fitting silk dress in smoky turquoise. Sixto went to every men's store in town looking for a shirt to match. It was an impossible color. Finally, to my great relief, he decided we didn't have to match.

My other tasks: Japanese lanterns for the strings of lights that would stretch over the tables in Toñita's front yard. Pink tablecloths for the ninety square tables Sixto had rented for the guests—he wouldn't hear of serving off metal tables that probably said "Corona" on them. He'd reserved white chair covers with big pink bows for the chairs, too. I bought a chocolate fountain, a portable steamer for the dresses, a tent awning to go over the head table where the quinceañera and her damas would sit for the reception, and a pink table skirt so it would look fancy from the front. We took miles of ribbons to decorate the church.

Most of the damas were cousins from Mexico, but Lucy wanted to invite four of her best friends to be damas as well. Their parents and some family friends wanted to go, too. Sixto presided over meetings to organize our caravan for the six-hundred-mile drive to Toñita's house. The trunk of every car and every open space in the van was crammed full of fancy dresses and decorations.

Our entourage included six teenagers—one was a brother of a dama—and ten adults. Each group of friends had been assigned to one of Tía Chayo's daughters' homes for the visit. Toñita's youngest son, Eduardo, gave up his room for Lucy and her girlfriends. Sixto and I were assigned to Toñita and Gavino's room. Toñita, Gavino, and Eduardo slept in the living room, elbowing into the small spaces between the plastic bags of paper plates, napkins, cups, and giant bottles of soda—name brand only, no generics. The dining-room table was covered with Ana's table decorations and boxes of the little plastic shoes.

The day before the big event, we drove into town to buy fruit for the chocolate fountain—pineapples, strawberries, bananas—and marshmallows. That evening, we ate dinner under the mango trees in Toñita's front yard. Our guests from Tucson included some vegetarians and vegans, but Toñita took that in stride, serving food that left us all stuffed and ready to lounge in comfort under the trees.

Sixto began reeling off the tasks remaining before the next day's big event. People nodded in a drowsy, after-dinner way.

Sixto took me aside. "There's a lot to do, mi amor," he whispered, "but everybody's just sitting around."

I laughed and left it to him to get people busy cutting fruit, stringing lights, and setting up the tent for the head table.

Gavino and his friends had slaughtered the pig that afternoon—an event our vegan friends took a drive to avoid hearing. Long after we went to bed, the men were talking low as they tended the cauldron of barbacoa they had buried deep in coals at the side of the house. Toñita told them in no uncertain terms that she didn't want to see any drinking, so they hid their bottles in paper bags. She didn't look too hard, and they made sure she didn't see anything as they kept vigil over the slow-simmering meat.

The transformation of Toñita's front yard continued early the next morning when a truck arrived with tables, chairs, and all those chair covers. Sixto and Eduardito began setting up the tables on each side so there was a plaza-like space in front of the head table. When they took off to decorate the church in Los Suárez, where the ceremony would be held, I was cutting the pink plastic tablecloths and tying the corners with ribbons. I wrapped a skirt around the head table and covered the top. Another one of Gavino's sisters—she was the neighbor on the opposite side from Luz Maria—brought over lush exotic plants to surround the head table. She had dug up enormous specimens of croton and vanilla from her yard and potted them in containers. They turned the space into a lovely garden setting.

The quinceañera chair—like something out of *Alice in Wonderland*—arrived with ribbons and bows and was placed right in the middle behind the table, where Lucy would have a regal view of her guests. The chairs for the damas, each covered in white with a pink bow, fanned out on either side. We had put lights around the awning the night before. The effect was amazing.

The bottom four feet of the mango trees were freshly coated with white paint that Toñita said would keep insects away, and the paper lanterns swung gently from above.

The girls were in Eduardo's room, where Toñita brought them breakfast and lunch as all these preparations were happening outside. Their sole job was to get beautiful. The hairstylist, with her portable salon, was providing them with curls and upsweeps. I could hear their laughter as I got started steaming our dresses.

It was a sound so sweet I wanted to bottle it. Later, there would be tears and complaints—because that, too, is what teenage girls are made of. But the joy in their voices as they got ready was like a bell ringing from a high hill. Pure, clear, and reverberating into the universe for all eternity.

That was the soundtrack of the quinceañera.

The bell-clear sound of adolescent girls laughing, the debate among cousins about the best way to attach a giant bow to the hood of our car, the clucking of tías in the kitchen as they finished macaroni salad and beans, and tíos rustling their paper sacks as they kept out of sight the things that must be kept out of sight.

Those were the sounds.

The silent hopes—the things we thought were so precious and fragile that they needed to be protected and sheltered—we carried in a box.

It contained the specially ordered Bible we would hand Lucy during the church ceremony. It had a bright pink cover with her name printed in gold. Joyful and a little frivolous at first glance, but solid and wise on the inside. Our gift, and our hope for her.

Our wishes for a fantastic life for our little girl were woven into every part of this day—and all the long months of preparations leading up to it. But just in case anybody missed the point, Sixto had amassed a stash of sparklers that would be handed out to the guests after dark. The bright and shining light, thrown high into the night, would be another reminder that her spirit was bright enough to light the way through any darkness.

The memories were in my mother's rhinestone necklace, which I wore above the too-deep neckline of my not-for-matrons fancy dress. The memories were also in the hard wooden pews where Sixto's mother had spent years praying for her children.

A quinceañera is a communal effort.

But it happens so fast that you can sometimes forget the point of it all.

That's why we hired a photographer.

He captured the moment when Lucy walked through the door of her tía's house, wearing that elegant dress with the impossibly big skirt, and holding her head just right to balance the tiara and all those curls. She squeezed into the back of our Nissan Sentra and we were off.

When we arrived at the church, I panicked.

There was nobody there except a few old ladies who looked like they never left.

The place was dressed up in ribbons and candles, and Lucy and the fifteen damas floated down the aisle on clouds of crinoline, satin, and lace.

But where were the guests? I couldn't believe we'd worked this hard for nothing. What about all those tables, set and waiting, at Toñita's house?

The damas adjusted their dresses and settled into a row of chairs on one side of the altar. On the opposite side, Sixto and I moved our chairs apart to make room for Lucy and her dress to sit between us. Our group of Tucson travelers settled in the empty sanctuary with puzzled looks. They, too, were wondering where everybody was.

It was a grand entrance without a grand audience.

Then the band started playing, and suddenly people flowed into the church in a steady and seemingly unending stream. Every seat was filled before the first song was done, and people stood shoulder-to-shoulder in the aisles. I could see a crowd peering in through the double doors at the back.

My chest began to swell with relief and anticipation. It was going to be okay. Then I remembered that I had forgotten to bring any Kleenex. I was sitting at the altar waiting for the start of one of the most emotional events in our daughter's life—and I'd forgotten tissues. I was the same woman who used to get weepy at Lucy's violin recitals. Sentimental was my middle name. There was no way I was going to make it through this without Kleenex.

A cousin sang a song. The band performed a song. Then Sixto and I presented Lucy with the pink Bible. I tried to choke out a few words, but I was lost. When I returned to my seat, I clamped my teeth into the inside of my cheek, hoping the pain would turn off the waterworks. I prayed for evaporation to stop the tears before they ran down my cheeks. Then I brushed them away with the back of my hand. Oh, for a tissue.

What saved me was a double cross.

We had a plan for the quinceañera, and a carefully orchestrated program that we'd printed out in two languages on beautiful pink paper to hand out to all the guests. As I mentioned, I was particularly pleased that Sixto's niece was going to officiate. It said so right in the program. This was my kind of symbolism. I am woman, hear me preach.

But when Maribel went to the lectern, she gave only a short greeting. Then she introduced her husband, and said he was going to give the message. I was so annoyed that my tears dried up on the spot.

So in retrospect, I guess she did me a favor.

After the message and more songs, Lucy kneeled on one of the satin pillows we'd brought while we and her damas surrounded her. We all put our hands on her head or shoulders and then the congregation surrounded us, laying their hands on our heads or shoulders in an ever-widening circle. After this blessing, we stepped aside to let Lucy and the damas make a procession out of church. The grand exit was well witnessed among murmurs of appreciation for the elegant gowns and queenly carriage of those young women.

The congregation followed and began the rounds of well-wishing. But the photographer put a quick end to that. He ushered the quinceañera party back inside for the photos by the altar.

Lots of photos. Lucy with all her damas. Lucy with each individual dama. Lucy with her parents. Lucy with tías. Then, after the rounds of well-wishing commenced again and finally finished, we drove to Toñita's neighbor's house to take more pictures in a patch of grass surrounded by flowers that made a beautiful background.

The light was fading as we arrived at Toñita's. As we got out of the car, a slight breeze washed over us like a cool kiss from my mother and Doña Sole. It freshened the evening and kept mosquitos away. The tables were full and rows of chairs had been set up behind them for overflow guests. A sustained cheer rose as we walked into the open space in front of the head table. Sixto and I stood on each side of Lucy as we walked in a circle with the damas following.

An old dog was sleeping in our path. I walked around. Everyone behind me also carefully changed course to avoid disturbing this old animal. No one kicked or yelled at the dog, which would have been the usual reaction in Mexico. As we approached on our second pass, Maribel went over to the dog and shooed it away. It was her second double cross of the day. But she did it gently enough so I let it pass. As odd as it may seem, I sensed the spirit of my mother in that old dog, and that's what my mother would have advised: let it pass.

Lucy and the damas took their place at the head table as boy cousins—in black pants, white shirts, and black ties—served them. Sixto and I made our way from table to table, greeting everyone, as more cousins served the guests.

The food was beyond just good. You could taste the love and the gratitude for a day devoted to joy. But it was the chocolate fountain that got people talking. The line to get to it snaked around the yard, and there were as many old people as young ones lining up twice.

On Toñita's orders, the men who wanted to drink stayed out of sight around the back of the house and kept their bottles under wraps. But when Porfirio arrived with his usual fanfare—no one expected him at the church—he drank his beer brazenly and lured some of the other men to join him in plain sight. He kept calling over to Sixto to ask when they would have the waltz. This was a Mennonite quinceañera, so the traditional father-daughter dance was not on the program. Porfirio must have known this. But he was a man who valued tradition and saw the restrictions of church as trivial. He wanted a waltz. But he didn't get it.

The Christian band played from a riser that had been built at the side of the house opposite the cooking pit. And there were games, too.

Lucy, her damas, and the other children dashed around, ducking through a human tunnel, dodging and laughing as people raised and lowered their arms. Lucy looked as happy as we had hoped she would be.

Lucy tossed her bouquet to a circle of not-yet-fifteen-year-old girls. We had brought a huge doll in a quinceañera dress that matched Lucy's. Our daughter gave that doll to the girl who caught the bouquet—it was a symbol of leaving her childhood behind. In the days when Sixto's mother was young, girls really did abandon childhood and begin building families at such young ages. Or sooner. Remember, Doña Sole was fourteen when she got married.

For us, there were tough years ahead as our daughter inched toward maturity.

At the end of the evening, Sixto passed out the sparklers.

People waved them around and threw them into the air at just the right moment so they would burn out before they hit the ground. Like riding in the back of the truck or swimming in street clothes or eating chicken that had been sitting on the stove all night, this was one of those things one did in Mexico without worrying about whether it was wise. The arc of the glittering sparklers heading up and then back to earth before blinking into darkness was simply beautiful. Nobody thought much about the consequences of having one of those burning wires land on you.

This was life, and life is both risky and unpredictable.

The next day some of us piled into trucks and headed for the beach. We found a hidden place that looked like no one had ever walked there. Pristine white sand. Not a soul in sight. I thought it was paradise. But after some discussion, those who knew the area best said it was better to find someplace else. I sputtered my objections. Sixto said they probably had their reasons. We wound up in a crowded but pleasant place where we could bob in the bathtub-warm water and squint up at the sun.

Lucy had a wonderful quinceañera.

The other goal—the effort to cheer Toñita—was only partially successful. Her sorrow continued to pour through the telephone. But that was only part of the problem. In addition to the pain, her calls were now filled with warnings—and they were like the germs of some terrible disease that infected Sixto.

Emilia's girls were getting into trouble. All three, Anayetzi, Daniela, and Tanya, got pregnant out of wedlock. Only Daniela married the boy, and then only after Emilia withheld her permission so long that everybody could see the reason for the wedding. Sixto was outraged after each phone call from Toñita bringing news of each pregnancy. He would hang up and say he was glad his mother had not lived to see such disgrace brought to her family. It was an ugly and utterly unforgiving pronouncement. But it wasn't the worst consequence.

Toñita's stories of each new horror came with the dark message: *ten cuidado con la niña.* Be careful with your girl. This warning incubated in Sixto's heart, completely bypassing his mind. Our daughter had been raised with far more structure and far more rules than Emilia's. She was a good kid. But he didn't give that a second thought.

Any interest Lucy showed in a boy became a disaster scenario in Sixto's mind. I'm sure many men build these doomsday visions of what will become of their daughters. But watching him watch her grow up was more than painful. He was going from the extreme of grief to the extreme of bad expectations. Both excesses involved people he loved more than his life.

In both cases, I was just a bystander. Nothing I said made any difference. I couldn't pull another quinceañera out of my purse.

He was taking classes at the university, and he said every time he heard young men laugh as they walked past him, he knew it was because they were mocking the girls with disrespect. Our daughter was still in high school, but her father's certainty that college boys were not to be trusted led to endless fights about Lucy's clothes. I wound up as the middleman, the go-between, and my patience was thin.

His concerns were pathological.

Lucy would dutifully have her potential boyfriends stop by the house to "meet the parents," and Sixto would sit on the couch wearing a look that said "Go ahead, make my day, punk." I would try to make small talk and lighten up the mood. Lucy would storm around. After a very few minutes, she would declare that it was time to go. They'd leave, and Sixto would spend the rest of the evening wandering to the front window to peer into the darkness. At least one of her boyfriends asked Lucy if her father was in the Mexican mafia. He looked that mean.

Instead of making her feel loved and protected, his attitude made her angry and secretive. She stopped bringing anybody around to the house. This, I thought, was far more dangerous; I felt more comfortable knowing whom she was seeing.

I longed for the Sixto I had married to return and send this nutty husband packing. Where was the man that my mother had praised as being so open and friendly? Why couldn't he be open and friendly now so Lucy would fill our house with her friends again, the way she had when she was younger? I missed the youthful energies as much as I missed that earlier version of my husband.

But it seemed to ease his mind when she stopped bringing boys home. He could pretend there were no boys. So we found an illusion of peace. That was a relief.

He had been there in the time of colic. Sane, stable, and knowing exactly what to do. I held things together as best I could in the teen years. Time did the rest.

Little by little, the pain of loss began to ebb. Grief let go. Little by little, Lucy began to remember that she once thought her parents were pretty cool. We grew together as a family again. Sixto even started to forgive God. Though I am sure he would say, "Oh, mi amor," if he heard me put it that way.

He still wouldn't go to church, though.

Our time wasn't peaceful or predictable as it had been in those preadolescent days of visits to grandmas on both sides of the border, and endless cycles of blissful, overdone holidays. Now we'd all tasted the fruit of the tree of the knowledge of good and evil. Death. Grief. Disappointment. Temptation. Anger. Betrayal.

The stuff that made Pancho Villa's death mask so ugly.

But there were also sparklers tossed high into a night sky.

Hope reflecting off the ocean's own reflection of an endless blue sky.

Love that endures the long sad years and the fast happy ones. Laughter. Hugs.

There is a heart-shaped stepping stone on the back patio into which Lucy inscribed the word "happy" when the concrete was soft enough to accept the message without resistance.

I don't know where bitter words and feelings go. They lurk in dark corners, and flee the broom. But eventually get swept away with the dust bunnies.

I do know that joy remains. It seeps into the walls and becomes part of the furniture. It lies down on the floor to make each next step a little easier.

Each spring the wildflowers come up in the front yard to remind me of the beauty all around. The beauty my mother taught me to love, and my husband helps me remember to notice. We're a team again. Not effervescent in that old way. But certainly not flat, either.

We make plans. We believe in miracles again, though we no longer believe we can make them happen at will.

CHAPTER TWENTY-TWO

I have one more celebration to tell you about, and then we're done.

It took place in a barn of a church in Los Mochis. A place big enough to accommodate the many families that would turn out for services on Sunday, but warehouse-simple to separate these plain-spoken believers from those who surrounded themselves with the ostentatious trappings of the Roman Catholic Church.

This church was about praising the Lord in passionate, tearful outbursts that were overseen by a preacher who dressed like everybody else. But this church—like many others—was also about being leased out to people from el otro lado who needed a place for a wedding or quinceañera.

In our case, it was a wedding.

And no preacher was needed. We brought our own: Manuel.

The church's homemade fabric banners were still hanging from the open-beam ceiling, with colorful letters urging people to *Crea en Dios*—Believe in God—and proclaiming that *Dios es amor*—God is love. But the wooden riser that served as an altar was surrounded with wedding flowers, and white tulle wrapped around railing on either side of the kneelers where the bride and groom would alternately listen to, and participate in, the ceremony.

After the music and the procession and the giving of the woman by her father to her groom, the couple sat side-by-side facing Manuel, who, as the family's official ordained minister, had been asked to preside over the ceremony. Sixto was up on the riser next to Manuel. He was the family's official translator.

The bride was Sixto's brother Pancho's daughter. The groom was a young American man who spoke no Spanish.

Pancho's family has lived in California for decades—legally, thanks to President Reagan's 1986 amnesty. Though born in Mexico, Pancho's children are as typically Californian as any I've ever met. Except for one thing. They were unabashedly committed to their family, and utterly unashamed about living at home years after many of their friends had moved to a more independent lifestyle. Among Mexican immigrants, the idea of a twenty-five-year-old still living at home is normal. After all, unless you are married, where else would you live? What's the point of living alone or with strangers when you have a perfectly good family to help and be helped by?

After Pancho's kids finished school and started working, they remained at home to help the family, which had long survived on the two jobs—sometimes three—that Pancho held at any one time. In Mexico, Pancho had been an accountant—when he could find work, which turned out to be too infrequently to raise a family. In the United States, he worked in food service or other low-skilled jobs. But here, the kids had a future. The family lived in a cramped two-bedroom apartment for many years. Eventually, thanks in part to the real-estate crash of 2008, they had enough saved up to buy a big house.

But that came later. When Pancho's daughter fell in love with a California gringo, they were still living in the little apartment.

Like our decision to have Lucy's quince in Mexico, Thelma and Jarod's decision to get married south of the border was all about family. In Los Mochis, they would have a wedding that included hundreds of relatives from both her mother and her father's families. The groom's family couldn't make it, so Jarod asked Sixto and me to stand up with him at the ceremony. Because he didn't speak much Spanish, Sixto was also pressed into service as translator.

This led to one of Sixto's finest hours—though only a few people in that church knew it.

We were all in our finery. I had a brown crepe skirt and satiny blouse with ruffles edged with tiny beads. It was the era of *Hairspray*, so I ratted my hair up high. Sixto had a new suit. Lucy was at her fashionista best. Thelma's dress was a fairy-tale white cloud, ordered in Mexico and custom made in yards and yards of elegance. After the procession, she took her place next to a dapper Jarod.

For his message, Manuel selected Bible verses that bolstered his thesis that God ordained men as heads of household, while women should be satisfied—honored—with supporting roles. His discussion of these verses made it clear that God wanted wives to obey their husbands in all things.

This was the natural order, he said. The secret to a happy marriage.

Sixto stirs his own coffee, so this message did not ring true to him. What's more, it was utterly contrary to everything he'd taught our daughter.

How was he going to handle this?

The dilemma was further complicated because Lucy and I weren't the only ones who would be able to understand both the Spanish and the English translation. Manuel understood quite a bit of English, and so did Pancho, though his wife, Aide, did not. The bride, her brother, and Manuel's two kids would also understand both the original and the translation.

It might have been my imagination, but I thought I saw a slightly triumphant look on Manuel's face as he passed the microphone to Sixto. He knew Sixto's views. The two of them had many philosophical discussions about such things over the years. Manuel was looking forward to hearing his words come out of Sixto's mouth.

Sixto took the microphone and established instant rapport with the group. He's always been comfortable speaking to a crowd, and he was ready to charm this group—even if only a few of them would understand what he said. He made eye contact around the room, building drama and waiting until he was sure everyone was paying attention.

Sixto has stage presence.

I'd seen him in action many times. But this time, I wondered if maybe he really was stalling for time.

Then he started with his usual bonhomie.

"We're all so happy to be here today to ask God to bless the marriage of these two wonderful young people."

He looked at the couple: "I know that you both understand that marriage isn't about one person being the boss and the wife doing just what she's told. It's about sharing your lives and respecting each other. There will be times when you might think it would be better if one of you just listened to the other, but that's not the way it is supposed to be. You are going to live your lives together and you need to make the important decisions in your lives together."

There must have been a crash when Manuel's jaw hit the floor. But nobody noticed. Thelma maintained her bride's face. The groom looked sincere and interested. He was paying attention to the only version of the speech he could understand.

As for Lucy, I had to resist the urge to give her a thumb's up on her papa's performance. But I did resist. She was seated behind me next to Manuel's daughter, and she told me later it was all she could do to keep a straight face.

I didn't dare look at Manuel.

Just like at Lucy's quinceañera, I bit the inside of my lip to keep my face from showing too much. This time it was a smirk, not tears, I needed to keep under control. The double cross at the altar this time was not a premeditated attempt to maintain the old social order. It was a spontaneous burst of honesty. I was savoring every second.

Sixto handed the mike back to his brother-in-law.

Manuel didn't look quite so triumphant anymore, but he maintained his calm, professional demeanor. If you didn't understand English, you wouldn't know anything unusual was going on.

Ana was no doubt proud to have both her husband and her brother sharing the honor of performing the ceremony. Her English isn't good enough to understand the translation, but she probably wasn't paying that much attention to Manuel's message, either. She might stir his coffee and serve his food. But even on that long-ago first visit, I had observed that Ana ran things in the family. She could have delivered a helpful sermon on the benefits of letting the man think he's in charge.

She has a generous heart, which goes a long way toward building a happy marriage. That's one of the things I learned from her over the years.

But it was Manuel who held the microphone. He was trying to regain control of the message.

He started with a caution: It was wrong—dangerously wrong—to try to put your own interpretation on the scriptures. No matter how modern someone might feel—no matter how sophisticated their life might have become on the other side of the border, for example—the Bible was clear. And the Bible said a happy marriage was a benevolent monarchy, not some misguided notion of equality.

Manuel passed the mike to Sixto for the next round of translation.

Sixto moved into the preacher's spot and paused so long that people looked up. Maybe they even lost the train of memories and dreams they'd been riding. He had their attention before he said a word. He spoke in a language that was understood only by about half-dozen of those present, but everybody listened.

He began by saying that God created both men and women with brains and ideas. It would be wrong for either of them not to use those God-given gifts. It would be wrong to let anybody—even somebody you loved—run your life. He talked about the joys of sharing decision-making. He said that if Thelma and Jarod one day had children, they might have differences of opinion about how those children should be raised. That was normal. What they had to do—what a loving God would want them to do—was talk to each other in mutual respect and come to a decision they both thought was right.

In a good marriage, he said, there are no bosses.

Then it was Manuel's turn again.

They are both good speakers. Both delivered their message with conviction and authority. Both commanded the attention of the congregation—at least when they began talking.

But people's minds wander and preachers always talk too long.

Nevertheless, it was a shame that more of those who were there that day didn't understand both sides of this dueling sermon. It certainly livened things up for those of us who did.

It is a tribute to both Manuel and Sixto that neither showed a hint of animosity during this odd display. Neither dropped the hopeful yet solemn attitude that's so important at a wedding. At one point Manuel tried to circumvent Sixto by speaking his part in English. But—like me with Spanish—he understands more than he can articulate. He had to revert to Spanish and let Sixto have the last word.

When the service was over, there was the usual rush to congratulate the happy couple. The heartfelt good wishes. The hugs and the weeping. Then there was the session with the photographer, who had taken no pictures during the actual ceremony, and now wanted everyone to go through the motions one more time so he could capture it in replay.

Thankfully, this reenactment did not include the sermons.

You might expect there would be some residual tension between Sixto and Manuel. If there was, I didn't see it. They were as cordial to each other as usual.

We all made our way to a big reception hall downtown that was decked out with white tablecloths, candles, an ice sculpture, and all the other amenities that seem so important when planning a wedding. Uniformed waiters stood by to serve us. This kind of party—for this many people—would have been unaffordable for a working-class family on the other side of the border. It was a grand affair.

Because Pancho's family is not Mennonite, the reception included drinking and dancing.

Sixto, Lucy, and I shared a big round table with some of the Mennonite contingent of the family, including Toñita and some of her children and grandchildren, and Ana and Manuel and their son. There was a steady stream of people coming to say hello to Sixto, and he was entertaining the table with jokes, as usual. In the United States, Sixto is usually quiet at parties. Not so in Mexico. Lucy and I had heard most of his jokes enough times that we began rolling our eyes well before the punch line. But we still laughed.

Our table was one of the loudest—at least until the waiter brought around a tray of glasses of beer. Then the silence fell like a brimstone curtain. This was the temperance table. Except for me. I would have preferred a glass of wine, but a beer looked pretty good.

Sixto knew it.

"Go ahead, mi amor," he said, as he saw me glance at the tray. "If you want."

My husband doesn't drink, but he often drives up to the store so I can have a glass of wine with dinner. This, however, was different. Toñita, who relegated the men to the shadows to do their drinking, was sitting right across the table.

She and others around that table had formed an impression of me over nearly two decades. I had earned a certain status just from longevity. They'd known me as the hopeless ninny who brought the wrong clothes and couldn't make tortillas. They watched me cut tile all day for Doña Sole's bathroom—and still not be able to make tortillas. They'd seen me devote myself to my daughter and make Sixto happy all these years. They accepted me as I was—jewelry, hair dryer, mosquito net, tea bags, bird-like appetite, single child.

I had nothing to prove.

If I took a beer, they would not suddenly change their opinion about me.

But they would feel slightly sorry for Sixto. Manuel would get back the triumphant look he'd worn at the church.

On the other hand, having a beer could put the cherry on the liberation cake. It would be a final finger flipped at Manuel's patriarchal view of the world—it would be the sassy answer I hadn't had the wit or nerve to give when he first asked me about the Egyptian disease all those years ago.

This was my dilemma.

In order to get the sense of just how offensive Manuel found drinking, consider this: Doña Sole came to visit us in the United States on two occasions. The first was when Sixto graduated from the University of Arizona. The second time was one year at New Year's.

She was not averse to a beer, and she and my mother shared several at a Mexican restaurant where we went to hear mariachis. (I know, I know. It's pretty strange to take a visiting Mexican to a Mexican restaurant. But this was Sixto's call.) But Doña Sole never had anything alcoholic to drink at our house.

We did take a picture of her holding a stemmed glass on New

Year's Eve, though.

When she returned to Mexico with that photo, Manuel was scandalized. He refused to help her make the trip to see us ever again. Now I suppose there were other male relatives who could have driven her to the airport, but his disapproval—based on a stemmed glass containing non-alcoholic sparkling apple cider— carried so much weight that she gave up future travel plans.

I had to factor that into my decision, too, as the waiter stood there waiting for my answer.

Manuel would win either way.

But I was not the same know-nothing little bride who'd blundered around trying to see in a blind mirror eighteen years ago. Now I could make things out clearly. What mattered was Sixto.

There was only one decision that would leave Sixto standing unchallenged on high ground.

I waved the waiter away.

Almost instantly the laughter returned to our table.

EPILOGUE

Our niece called from Nogales, Sonora, the other day. This is Rosi, the daughter of Jilberto and Clara.

Rosi and her family used to live in Tucson, but they left during the great recession, which was also the era of great hatred in Arizona, when laws designed to intimidate undocumented immigrants were popular.

Rosi and her husband Alberto did not leave because of the hostile environment created by opportunistic politicians—even though the mood scared Rosi during their last months in this country. They left because work dried up. After the real-estate crash, there was much less demand for granite countertops, and cutting granite is what Alberto did.

For the record, they did not enter the country illegally. They and their two young sons have visas. Their little girl was born a US citizen. But they lived here in violation of the terms of those tourist visas, and Alberto was not supposed to be working.

Nobody really cared until a bunch of hateful politicians decided to rouse people's fear and direct it at hardworking families.

Long before that happened, Rosi's family was part of ours, and her family enriched our lives. Unlike most of Sixto's family, we could see them regularly.

And we did.

We went to their apartment to eat Rosi's *mole* and Alberto's carne asada, while watching pirated movies that Alberto bought for his big-screen TV. (He had the blockbusters the day they opened in theaters.) We hosted big birthday parties for the kids at our house. On other, more grown-up celebrations, Alberto played bartender, making margaritas with generous portions of tequila and fresh key limes.

Alberto made good money doing expert work for a company that didn't worry about whether his work documents were authentic. He was a good husband and a generous father; payday meant buying stuff for the kids, as well as restocking the kitchen. Rosi has a naturally sunny disposition. She raised her children to be respectful, but took plenty of time to laugh at their antics along the way. She enjoys motherhood for its own sake.

Rosi got scared after Alberto was stopped by the police one evening for driving around a speed bump near their apartment. Everybody always drove around that speed bump, she said. She knew they were looking for a reason to stop Alberto. He had his visa, so they let him go. But if they saw him there regularly, they would know he was living here.

Rosi heard stories about parents being deported and separated from their US-born children. These were not news stories. These were stories about people she knew.

She was in constant fear about her baby. As a US citizen, the baby could not legally be put across the line with her parents. She asked me what to do. I was honest. I assured Rosi that we would take the little girl and bring her to Mexico if the family was deported. But I also knew *La Migra* might not give Rosi the chance to call us. This pampered princess of a baby might wind up in state custody and out of our reach.

That worried all of us. It terrified Rosi. She stopped going out, except to walk her oldest son to elementary school. The once-pleasant trip with her baby in a carriage and her youngest son tagging along became an ordeal. She was on constant alert.

When school was out, they left for Mexico.

Alberto and the boys were sorry to go. Rosi was relieved, and so was I. Living here was too risky.

They decided to settle in Nogales, because that's where Alberto's parents lived. We helped them buy a sliver of land on the collapsing edge of a wash in one of the *colonias* south of the urban center. Alberto hired a man with a big truck to bring in load after load of fill dirt to create a ledge on his sliver of land. He reinforced it with tires. Then he used scraps of wood and other materials to build a few rooms for them to live in.

Their house was sturdier and far more aesthetically pleasing than many of the others that clung to the hills around that wash. It was home.

Rosi no longer had to worry about being separated from her little girl. She was content, even without the conveniences she'd enjoyed in her modern American apartment. She cooked on a tiny butane-powered stove and washed dishes without indoor plumbing—just like Doña Sole had done so many years before.

Rosi's water came from a tank on the roof. A man refilled it periodically—and for a price—from a tanker truck that he drove up and down those steep dirt roads on a regular schedule. Alberto's plan was to retrofit his father's old truck as a tanker so they could go into the water business, selling door-to-door in another colonia that didn't have service.

But that fell through.

Then Alberto was going to make furniture; he was an artist and did exquisite work. But there was nobody to buy it. Everybody in the colonia was as poor as they were. The *maquiladoras* weren't hiring then.

Alberto's skills included carpentry, drywall, masonry, cement work, tile setting, auto mechanics, and, of course, precision granite cutting. Except for plumbing, there was never a problem around our house that Alberto didn't volunteer to fix—and fix right. But there were no paying jobs for his skills in Mexico.

Alberto still had his visa, so he would make occasional trips to the United States to do odd jobs for individuals. Mostly ironwork—another of his skills.

He and the boys pined for their life in the United States. They still had their big TV and the world's largest collection of DVDs to remind them of better days. But life was much, much different in Mexico. Harder. Less fun. There were no fast-food restaurants, let alone money to buy junk food. No payday trips to the swap meet. No electric car to drive around the parking lot of the apartment complex.

Rosi started making popsicles in her freezer and selling them to the neighbor kids for a few pesos. Business was good. She and

Alberto began making supply runs to the United States to buy groceries that could be sold for a profit in the colonia. With their visas and their car, they had mobility that many of their neighbors lacked. They made the most of those resources.

Alberto built an addition to the house as a storefront. Rosi's store had a counter and a flap that could be pulled down and secured from the inside when she closed up shop. I had a plastic banner made for her: *Tiendita Los Betos*. Rosi hung it outside when she was open.

A bakery said they would supply Rosi with goods on credit; she could pay after she'd sold them. They were on their way. The little store gave them cash to live on. They owned the house and land. Alberto did odd jobs here and there.

But as the recession got worse, the attitudes against Mexican workers turned uglier and people began to be afraid to hire him. Several jobs fell through. One guy refused to pay after two weeks of full-time labor.

Instead of being able to set aside the money from the store to buy new merchandise, they had to spend what they made to buy food, water, and gas for the stove.

Then they ran out of things to sell. We gave them money to stock up again. But the pattern kept repeating.

When Rosi called, she told Sixto that they closed the little store. She had to tell the bakery she couldn't sell their goods anymore because she was afraid she wouldn't be able to make good on the credit they extended. The car had finally quit running—despite the new engine Alberto put in—so they couldn't make the trip across the border to pick up the free produce they'd been getting. She didn't have anything to sell. The boys were starting school next week . . . and . . . well . . .

I could hear Sixto's end of the conversation, and I knew she was asking for money. Not asking, exactly, but hinting broadly. I knew it was a last resort, because Rosi is a hard worker and so is Alberto.

I also knew times were tough for us, too. Sixto told her that. Our daughter was at the university and tuition had gone up rapidly. The money we'd saved to pay for her college was gone before she finished her sophomore year. Because of unpaid furloughs and increased medical-insurance costs, Sixto's salary was shrinking, and so was mine. Our savings dwindled as the credit-card bill grew.

But we weren't poor.

When I heard Sixto tell Rosi we could only afford to bring them a few notebooks and pencils, I knew it was true. Technically. But it was hard to hear him say that because I didn't want it to be true. I wanted to help.

After he hung up, we played gin rummy at the kitchen table with Mona Lisa cards we bought in Paris several years earlier on our trip to Europe.

We had so much, I said.

"What if we get to the gates of heaven and they ask 'Why didn't you help them?'" I said, as he picked up the pile and laid down a jack, a ten, and a nine of hearts.

"I don't want to feel guilty, mi amor," he said. "Maybe Alberto just needs to get moving."

"But maybe there is nothing he can do."

We talked about how we really needed to get our own finances in order. We couldn't spend our seed corn to help other people.

Besides, helping didn't always help.

After Emilia's daughter Anayetzi had her baby, she withdrew to a dark bedroom in Emilia's house. It was a terrible situation for her, and worse for the baby, whom she'd named Soledad.

Sixto had many phone calls with Toñita and Ana, and much discussion about what to do.

We agreed to put up the money for Anayetzi to attend beautician school, and Ana agreed to let Anayetzi and the baby live with them in Ciudad Obregón while she studied. It was a solid, legitimate opportunity to build a life. She did well in school. The baby thrived with Ana's attention.

But when Anayetzi finished studying, she took that baby and went right back to that dark bedroom in Emilia's house. She didn't use the expensive skill her tíos helped her acquire.

"It's possible," I said, "that we could get to the gates of heaven and God would say, 'Why didn't you let them learn for themselves?' It's possible."

"It's possible," he said.

"But I kind of doubt it."

I was still the great would-be fixer of all things.

So we said we'd sleep on it and decide the next morning whether to borrow money on our credit card to help Rosi and Alberto and their beautiful children.

Sixto won big at the card game, and we went to bed after watching *House Hunters International* and wondering how this very young couple came up with a million-plus dollars to buy a place on the French Riviera.

Must not have any Mexican relatives, I thought.

About 2:00 a.m., the phone rang. I held my breath as Sixto rushed into the kitchen and said hello.

I heard the fear in his voice—a fear he tried to mask with false cheerfulness: "What is it, *mi niña?*" It was Lucy.

This was the call in the night that every parent fears.

I heard lots of "okay" and "yes" and other such comments. Then he said he'd be right there and hung up. My blood ran cold.

"What's wrong?" I said. I was in the kitchen, too, by now.

He was rummaging in the junk drawer.

"Javelinas," he said. "She can't get up the driveway. Where's the flashlight?"

Thank heaven. This was the Miracle of the Not-so-bad Crisis.

Javelinas frequent our front yard, especially in the late summer and early fall. They browse a few of the plants that overhang the flowerpots and move on to the palo verde beans in our neighbor's yard. They don't bother you if you don't bother them. But they are big and so are their tusks. They will charge at dogs and others foolish enough to get in their way.

Sixto was ready to rush into a herd of eight or nine in order to rescue his daughter, who was safely sitting in the car at the end of the driveway.

"You can't go out there," I said.

So there was a discussion. I insisted she could just wait and stood between him and the front door.

I prevented him from executing the rescue he'd been ready to mount on her behalf ever since she reached puberty—although the villains in his imagination were always human, not peccary.

In disgust with my interference, he went around to the back

gate, which opens directly onto the driveway, and shined the light on the now-retreating herd. Our child drove up and he went out to bring her up to the gate.

The drama was over, but the two of them acted as though she had just escaped the most perilous threat.

I congratulated them on their bravery and went back to bed.

Before the weekend was over, Sixto and I broke down and decided to rescue Rosi and her family, too. Even though they might have been able to wait for better times, just as Lucy could have waited out the javelinas.

We used the credit card to buy school supplies and grocery staples. Sixto took a little money out of the bank and met Rosi and the two boys in Nogales, Arizona. There he used the credit card again to buy them new shoes and belts.

The boys also had a few words of advice from their tío Sixto about the importance of studying and rejecting the temptations of growing up in a poor colonia. He told Rosi that when we get caught up with the bills we might be able to help her stock the store again.

I subsequently took Rosi shopping when they borrowed a car and drove up to see us.

She always thanked me profusely, and I always said not to mention it. I meant that.

My life was enriched by marrying a man that my country refused to allow to enter by the front door. The lives of my family and friends were enriched.

His family was a gift to me.

His journey through our labyrinth culture has been fun, and sometimes painful to share.

Sixto took the culture and values he brought with him—the Old World of ideas that so appalled his teenage daughter and frustrated me—added the education and knowledge he gained here, and devoted his time to enriching the lives of countless students in his classes.

His example empowered their parents—most of them Latino, some of them probably undocumented immigrants—to knock on the principal's door and become involved in their children's education. That's budding civic engagement that will make a difference in their children's lives, and will help the United States move toward a more perfect Union.

That's the face of the immigrant experience that I know. It's a beautiful, multifaceted reality that is more interesting than the stereotypes.

And just to shoot down one lingering stereotype: Alberto did find work at one of the maquiladoras shortly after we bailed them out the last time.

His skill as a machinist made him a six-day-a-week employee. I don't know how much they pay him—it's likely far less than what he earned in this country. But he's feeling good about himself. He's rebuilding their house into a bigger, better, two-story model.

These days, when Rosi calls, it's to talk about news of the children—their success at school. She also expresses her gratitude for the help we gave them. She says the food I bought her on the last shopping trip we took together was nearly gone when Alberto got the job. She wants me to know how much it meant to her family. I tell her not to mention it.

I did tell Sixto, however, that I am prepared to remind whoever is watching the gates of heaven on Judgment Day that I bought the large size of everything when I took Rosi shopping.

He said, "Oh, mi amor."

In the meantime, we have a new tradition of visiting Rosi and Alberto on Christmas Eve Day to share Rosi's good cooking and watch the kids break a piñata.

One year, we got a different lesson—as Sixto would say—in how trying to help out can backfire.

Some do-gooder from this side of the line had taken outdated food down to the colonia to pass out to the people. It was a nice gesture, and Rosi was thankful. She got a share of the bounty and put it aside for our visit. But when she tried to make *buñuelos* that Christmas Eve, something went seriously wrong. They just wouldn't fry up right.

She tossed out that dough, and Sixto mixed up another batch. His didn't work, either.

Alberto also tried. Also without success.

It was my turn.

I picked up the bag of flour: self-rising, it said in English.

No wonder it didn't work, I said.

After a good laugh, Rosi sent the boys to borrow some regular flour. Before long, we were eating our deep-fried treat with honey drizzled over it.

The secret is using the right ingredients.